A TASTE OF Shan

A TASTE OF Shan

A culinary and photographic expedition
through the Shan province of northern Myanmar

PAGE BINGHAM

Marshall Cavendish
Cuisine

The author will be donating her royalties from the sale of this book to the Foundation for the People of Burma, an organisation that provides humanitarian aid to the people of Myanmar.

Design by Lynn Chin Nyuk Ling
Food photography by Romana Vysatova
All other photographs by Page Bingham

Published by Marshall Cavendish Cuisine
An imprint of Marshall Cavendish International
1 New Industrial Road, Singapore 536196

Other Marshall Cavendish Offices:
Marshall Cavendish Ltd. 5th Floor, 32-38 Saffron Hill, London EC1N 8FH, UK • Marshall Cavendish Corporation. 99 White Plains Road, Tarrytown NY 10591-9001, USA • Marshall Cavendish International (Thailand) Co Ltd. 253 Asoke, 12th Flr, Sukhumvit 21 Road, Klongtoey Nua, Wattana, Bangkok 10110, Thailand • Marshall Cavendish (Malaysia) Sdn Bhd, Times Subang, Lot 46, Subang Hi-Tech Industrial Park, Batu Tiga, 40000 Shah Alam, Selangor Darul Ehsan, Malaysia

Marshall Cavendish is a trademark of Times Publishing Limited

National Library Board Singapore Cataloguing in Publication Data

Bingham, Page.
A taste of Shan : a culinary and photographic expedition through the Shan province of northern Myanmar / Page Bingham. – Singapore : Marshall Cavendish Cuisine, c2009.
p. cm.
ISBN-13 : 978-981-4276-32-0

1. Cookery, Burmese. 2. Shan (Asian people) – Food – Burma.
3. Shan (Asian people) – Burma – Social life and customs. I. Title.

TX724.5
641.59591 -- dc22   OCN424911213

Printed in Singapore by KWF Printing Pte Ltd

Contents

acknowledgements

I would like to express my deepest appreciation to all the people who made this book possible. Without their invaluable help and support, I would never have been able to write this book:

All the Shan people who took the time to give me their delicious recipes.

My sister, Daisy Helman, for never losing faith in me.

Sara Rooney, for your inspiration and enthusiasm.

Sarah Adler, for being a great friend and getting me to Myanmar in the first place!

Leslie Maglitta, without your help, this project would never have materialised.

Sebastian Stuart, for listening to what I had to say and putting it into words.

Sharyn Bahn, for your wisdom.

Daphne Hays, chef extraordinaire.

Pote Videt, whose helping hand opened so many doors for me.

Romana Vysatova, master photographer, for your brilliant eye in capturing the essence of my recipes.

Molly Anathan Hamilton for designing the map of Myanmar used in this book.

Sai Aung Tun, for steering me in the right direction, for your wonderful recipes and your spirited cooking lessons.

Sai Khin Maung, my trusty guide and translator who made my travels in Shan state possible.

My mom and dad.

My husband, Jim Anathan, for all your love, support and patience.

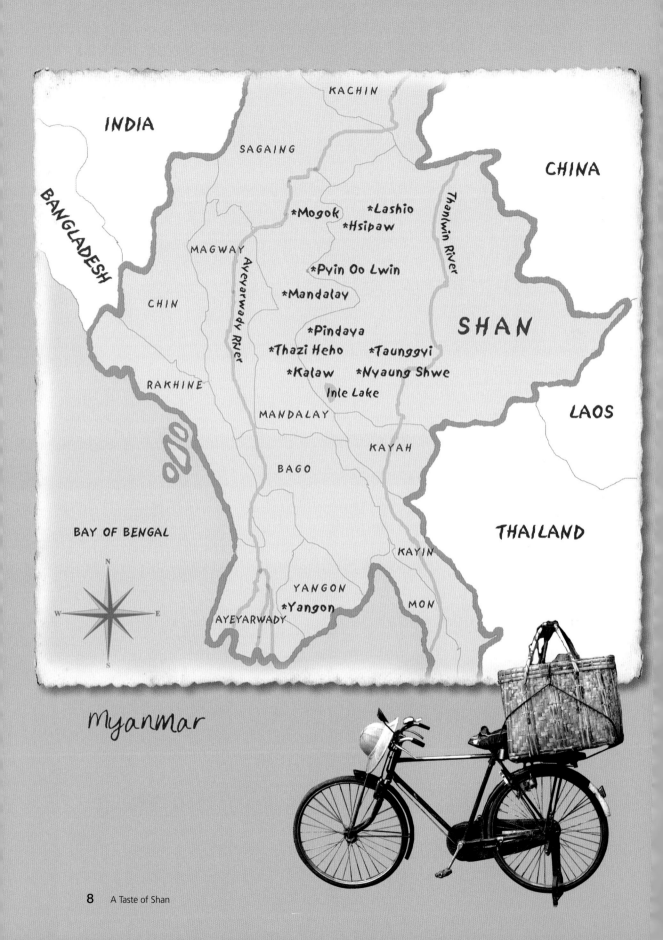

INDIA

BANGLADESH

CHINA

KACHIN

SAGAING

MAGWAY

CHIN

*Mogok   *Lashio
          *Hsipaw

Thanlwin River

*Pyin Oo Lwin

*Mandalay

SHAN

*Pindaya
*Thazi Heho   *Taunggyi
  *Kalaw   *Nyaung Shwe
        Inle Lake

RAKHINE

Ayeyarwady River

MANDALAY

LAOS

KAYAH

BAGO

BAY OF BENGAL

THAILAND

KAYIN

N
W   E
S

YANGON
*Yangon

MON

AYEYARWADY

Myanmar

Preface

Shan cooking saved my marriage.

At home in Cambridge, Massachusetts, my husband and I had hit a rough patch. We were both experiencing the seven-year itch, and there was some scratching going on. We decided to separate, at least temporarily. I found an apartment nearby and moved in. There I was, at loose ends and nursing a broken heart when an email arrived from my dear friend Sara, who was in Yangon, Myanmar researching her doctorate on medical anthropology. She invited me over for a visit. It took me about a second to reply with an emphatic "Yes!". I would try a change of scenery; or more to the point, a geographical cure.

I didn't know a lot about Myanmar, except that it was in Southeast Asia and ruled by a military junta. My imagination conjured up vague images of scowling soldiers, tribal villages, whispered intrigue, mystical temples and jungles filled with tigers, monkeys and elephants. The day after Sara's invitation, I filled out a form on the Myanmar government web site and sent my passport to the Myanmar consulate in New York. Within days, I got it back, stamped with a tourist visa.

Barely 24 hours after getting my visa, I found myself bleary eyed and jet-lagged, in the Yangon International Airport, surrounded by swirling swarms of people laden with everything from suitcases to live animals. Was a bleating baby goat considered carry-on luggage in Myanmar? Dazed, sweat-soaked and with my feet swollen to elephantine proportions, I began to question my sanity. What on earth had I gotten myself into? Was I really that miserable back in Cambridge? In the midst of my second-guessing, I spotted Sara. I hugged her as if she were a life raft.

In Shan state, the women and children typically dress in bright colours. I was told that they love bright colours because of the cold weather—vivid colours bring 'sunshine' into their lives. And this is reflected in the demeanour of the people. It is not uncommon to see groups of people laughing and smiling as they went about their daily tasks in the markets or relaxed in the tea shops, chatting.

The endearing faces of the people of Shan. They adorn their faces with *thanakha*, a paste made from ground bark. This bark comes from several different kinds of trees that grow primarily in central Myanmar. *Thanakha* smells a bit like sandalwood and is thought to be beneficial in helping with acne and other skin conditions, although the Shan apply it mainly in a decorative fashion (this is especially so among the children), or as a sunscreen to protect against the harsh rays of the sun.

Sara guided me expertly through the throngs and out to a waiting car, which took us to my hotel. Although all I wanted was a shower and a bed, she insisted on a welcoming lunch at The Strand, the city's best hotel, telling me it was a ritual for new arrivals. I mustered what little energy I had left and agreed. Off we set on one of the most challenging walks of my life—down serpentine streets, dodging trishaws, bikes, cars, stray dogs and onrushing people, past monks draped in saffron and burgundy robes, cluttered tea shops and food stalls that spilled onto the streets, outdoor markets selling dazzling flowers and colourful fruit and vegetables—the whole panorama accompanied by a raucous urban cacophony and the smell of *ngypai* or fermented prawn paste, a base ingredient in Burmese curries.

As we dodged yet another speeding car, it hit me: I was a long way from Boston. This was quickly followed by another epiphany: I'd forgotten about my jet lag, my exhaustion and even my swollen feet. I felt exhilarated, alive and ravenous to experience all that Myanmar had to offer... except maybe lunch at The Strand hotel. I explained to Sara that I could have a fancy hotel lunch anywhere in the world, and that I would much rather be a little more adventurous. She suggested that we try Shan food and I readily agreed, although all I knew was that the Shan were one of Myanmar's many ethnic minorities. Sara led us to a tiny, cramped restaurant tucked away in an alley, its air filled with a fragrant, heady mix of ginger, garlic and shallots. We perched ourselves on tiny stools and were greeted by the proprietress, a demure young woman dressed in a bright green shirt and an orange *longyi*. (I quickly learned that the Shan love bright colours.) She had shiny jet-black hair, wore red lipstick and her cheeks were painted with large circles of *thanakha*, a tan-coloured paste that the men and women of Myanmar adorn their faces with, both for beauty and for protection from the sun.

A parade of dishes began to appear from the miniscule kitchen. First came deep-fried Shan rolls stuffed with tofu and bean sprouts, flavoured with coriander and accompanied by a spicy vinegar dipping sauce. The play of textures was exquisite, with the crisp bite of the roll giving way to the soft moist tofu and gentler crunch of the sprouts, all of it infused first with the tart vinegar and then the bold dusky coriander. Next came a broth flavoured with green chillies, garlic and ginger, its revivifying aroma and dense flavour were somehow comforting, in that way soup often is. Then came fish steamed in banana leaves, flavoured with a hint of tamarind—flaky, white and melt-in-the-mouth tender. The fish was accompanied by the most divine green beans I had ever tasted, lightly stir-fried with fresh tomatoes and shallots. Between dishes, we were encouraged to cleanse our palates by sipping hot Shan tea, a green tea with a slightly nutty flavour. Sitting there on that tiny stool, savouring one dish after another, I was transported to a world of sensual delight. I'm sure my state of mind had something to do with it, but this was the most delicious meal of my life.

When I finally hit my hotel bed, I was happier than I had ever been in many months. Who needs a husband when you have a new culture and cuisine to discover? I spent the next several days learning everything I could about the Shan people and rummaging through bookstores in search of a Shan cookbook. There was none to be found. Sara suggested I try one more place, an old bookstore across town, but warned that the owner could be crotchety. Since I now adored exploring the streets of Yangon, I took up the challenge. The Bagan bookstore was musty and smelled slightly of mould. The proprietor was a tiny man in his seventies, wearing a faded *longyi* loosely wrapped around his waist and old flip-flops. He sat behind a desk piled high with books and acknowledged my entrance with a slight raising of his eyebrows. I gingerly nosed around, being careful to replace everything just as I found it. There were a lot of fascinating books, but no Shan cookbook. Just as I turned to leave, he stood up, smiled, and asked me what I was looking for. When I told him, he said, "But there are no Shan cookbooks. You should write one!" "Me!" I blushed, "I don't know anything about Shan cuisine, much less writing a cookbook!" "Don't let that stop you," he enthused, "just go meet the Shan and write down their recipes. Then, I can sell it here!" I smiled at the idea, thanked him, and he sent me on my way with, "Good luck, I'll be waiting!"

Inspired by his spontaneous encouragement and eager to throw myself into a project, I began to investigate Shan food and the Shan people, whose native region is in central eastern Myanmar, bordering China, Thailand and Laos. My quest started in Yangon and took me to the cities and regions of Mandalay, Inle Lake, Hsipaw, Lashio and Taunggyi. It took me to restaurants, cafes, tea shops, markets and roadside stands, and into the kitchens of welcoming Shan families. I soon had a notebook filled with delicious and exotic recipes. I learned about Shan history and culture. I made new friends and immersed myself in a different world, one in which I was often the only Westerner.

What I had planned as a short reprieve from my problems at home stretched into a seven-month adventure. When it was over, I not only had enough recipes for a cookbook, I had a new sense of myself as curious, capable and moving-forward in my life. And something else happened as well. As I inhaled a bowl of fragrant rice and fish standing beside a dusty road, or sat down to an elaborate meal in a family's dining room, I would be struck by how much I wanted to share the adventure with my husband. On those occasions when I could find an Internet connection, I excitedly told him of my discoveries and he responded with enthusiasm and support. By the time I arrived back home, we had a gained a new appreciation for each other and we reconciled.

I'm not promising that the recipes in this book will save your marriage or perform any other miracles, but I hope they will awake you to a new culture, and your palate to new and exciting sensations.

The Yangon train station is filled with action all hours of the day. It's a hub not only for workers commuting into Yangon from the outskirts of the city, but also for long-distance travellers journeying from the far ends of Myanmar, and their flocks of animals as well! Besides commuters and travellers, hawkers selling anything, from food and flowers to household necessities, also contribute to the lively bustle at the train station.

Introduction

Once I had decided to write a cookbook on Shan recipes, the question became: "Where do I begin?"

The Shan state is large, containing almost a quarter of Myanmar's land, but contains no major cities where I could establish a comfortable and convenient base from which to explore. An English friend in Yangon, Emma, suggested I consider Mandalay, a city of just under a million people that sits 724 kilometres (450 miles) north of Yangon, very near the border of the Shan state. Emma was heading there to research a book she was writing on George Orwell, who had been stationed in Mandalay when he was a member of the Indian Imperial Police from 1922 to 1927, and whose first novel, *Burmese Days*, was based on this experience. Emma convinced me that Mandalay made all the sense in the world because of its location, because it was home to many Shan, and because it was a lovely and lively city.

So after packing my bags, buying my train ticket, and saying my farewells to friends—especially the encouraging bookstore owner who was thrilled I was taking his advice—off I set. As Emma and I rode through the sweltering streets of Yangon in a rickety trishaw expertly driven by a man older than my grandfather, she warned me that I should prepare myself to be a 'bit' uncomfortable for the next 16 hours. As soon as we arrived at the train station, I got a taste of what she meant. It made the chaotic Yangon airport look like a Zen monastery. There were dogs running about; women in brightly coloured *longyis* selling food from metal containers, which sat on trays perfectly balanced on top of their heads; men hawking everything from cigarettes to newspapers to toys; young girls offering garlands of jasmine flowers to be worn around the neck; a slew of beggars pawing for money; and packs of small children attaching themselves to you in hope of a little treat. As we made our way through the station, I was repeatedly pinched or tapped on the shoulder. I quickly learned that this was their way of getting your attention, but I never got over being startled by this custom. Scores of times as I was going about my business, I would suddenly receive a firm pinch!

Through the noise and chaos, Emma's chirpy British voice kept reminding me to "hurry along, the train to Mandalay won't wait!" My clothes were sweat-plastered to my body and I was constantly fighting off pinching beggars and children. I wanted to scream! The more-experienced Emma shooed them away as best she could, took me by the arm and firmly guided me to our platform.

Once onboard the train, relief washed over me, until I saw our seats. 'First class' consisted of narrow wooden benches packed with passengers. When these were filled to bursting, the aisles became the perch of choice. Two rows behind us were cages filled with roosters, and judging by their non-stop squawking, they were even less comfortable than we were. Air conditioning? Dream on. You could open the windows, which was a blessing since everyone was smoking up a storm. When we finally pulled out of the station, there was a mass clamber to the windows to wave goodbye to loved ones. The swell of bodies literally carried me with them and I found myself packed like a sardine with my head sticking out the window. Well, at the least, the evening air was a little cooler. When I finally settled in next to Emma, she entertained me by reading Kipling's poem, *The Road to Mandalay*, as we headed into the fiery sunset.

"Elephints a-pilin' teak
In the sludgy, squdgy creek,
Where the silence 'ung that 'eavy
you 'arf afraid to speak!
On the road to Mandalay..."

I don't know what road Kipling took, but I was positive it wasn't this train. Silence was a distant memory and sleep was pretty much out of the question. But after a bumpy, stifling night, we arrived safely early the following morning.

Once again, my exhaustion fell away—it was immediately obvious that Mandalay, Myanmar's second largest city, was far more genteel and laid-back than Yangon. The train station was less chaotic and the ride to our guesthouse took us down wide boulevards filled with bicycles and trishaws, past graceful temples and quiet streets lined with lovely houses, flower beds and graceful trees. Because it was the capital of the last independent Burmese kingdom in the mid 19th century, and remains an important Buddhist centre today, Mandalay is filled with pagodas, monasteries and palaces.

We arrived at our guesthouse. It was clean and comfortable, with large rooms and a deck that was perfect for watching the sunset. The guesthouse was northeast of the city centre, near the palace of the last Burmese royal family and Mandalay Hill. The royal palace was destroyed in the Second World War, but faithfully reconstructed in the 1990s and is a popular tourist attraction. Mandalay Hill rises dramatically, almost 0.2 kilometres (800 feet) from the Mandalay Plain and is a Buddhist holy site. Legend has it that Buddha visited Mandalay Hill and prophesied that a great city would grow up around it. Thousands of pilgrims visit its many pagodas and monasteries every year.

I quickly fell in love with Mandalay and spent many happy hours exploring its streets and monuments. It is an enchanting place filled with amazing examples of Southeast Asian architecture and friendly people. And because of the Buddhist influence, it has a tranquility that was a balm to my harried soul. The city is also known for its intellectual vitality and tea shops are a way of life here, comparable to the cafés of Paris. People of all ages sit around tiny sidewalk tables having lively discussions, sipping sweet, rich tea made with condensed milk and eating fried dough sprinkled with sugar and cinnamon and sometimes topped with banana; some variation of this fattening treat seems to be universally popular around the globe, but somehow, sitting in a Mandalay tea shop, I felt less guilty indulging. Mandalay also has wonderful morning markets and many Shan restaurants. Emma was right, it was the perfect base for my exploration of Shan cuisine.

I quickly made friends and contacts. One of them was a Shan woman named Harriot, a friend of Emma's, whose husband built wooden puppets. They lived on a pretty street near the centre of town, in an airy open house shared with her extended family. On our first visit, Emma and I sat on the front porch. Harriot served us tea and told us she was going to make us her favourite Shan dish, rice salad.

Tea shops in Yangon are great places to indulge in sweet treats with a cup of tea. Tea shop boys (pictured above) run the tea shops and make some of the best teas in all of Myanmar!

Trishaws and bicycles are common forms of transport in Myanmar. They carry everything from live animals to blocks of ice. Bicycles are especially popular in Mandalay where there tends to be more bicycles than cars.

Inle Lake is the second largest natural lake in Myanmar. It is a shallow lake, with a depth of only 3 metres (10 feet) in some places. Covered with reeds and aquatic plants, the Intha people have devised a special technique of rowing their boats with their legs. The Intha fish for carp in the lake (top left) and build their houses on wooden piles driven deep into the lake bed (pictured above).

A woman preparing a dish of Squeezed Rice with Fish (*Htamin Gyin*) at the Four Sisters Inn in Inle Lake.

It was always a treat watching people returning from the morning market. There would be women carrying basketfuls of produce on their heads, families on bicycles loaded with everything but the kitchen sink, and children scurrying about. If not walking, riding their bicycles or taking a ride in a trishaw, they could be enjoying a bumpy ride home on a horse or donkey cart.

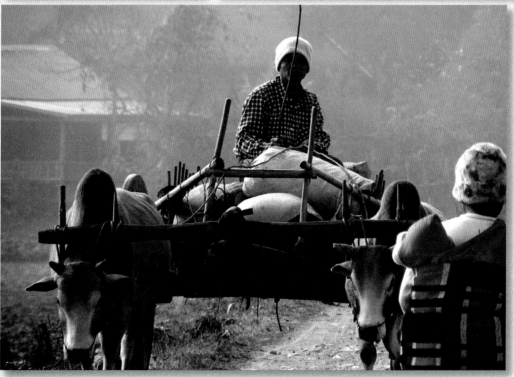

She also told us a little bit about Shan history. Thought to have originally migrated from the Yunnan province in China, the Shan, who are Buddhists, ruled most of what is now Myanmar from the 12th century through the mid 16th century. They were then conquered by native Burmese, who ruled until the British took control in 1885. In 1947, Myanmar gained independence from Britain, with the Shan state granted the right to secede after 10 years. When that day arrived, the central government in Yangon revoked the right. This led to the Shan liberation movement, which still exists today, with Shan rebel fighters concentrated in the eastern mountains bordering Thailand. During flare-ups in the ongoing civil war, Shan villages are burned and their inhabitants displaced. In order to ensure that they do not join the rebel forces, young Shan men are often conscripted into the army or into forced labour on the country's roads. To escape this, many young men flee to Thailand, and the Shan royal prince lives in exile in Canada.

When Harriot excused herself to prepare our lunch, Emma led me to Harriot's husband's workshop to look at the puppets. They were wondrous creations, beautifully carved with painted faces giving way to exquisite costumes made of cotton and silk and embroidered with pearls and stones. He showed us how the puppets are manipulated by strings hanging from a small wooden pallet, and explained that they represent characters from Buddhist legends and from *Ramayana*, the ancient Sanskrit epic poem. *Ramayana* tells the story of a prince whose wife is abducted by a demon, and explores themes of good, evil and karma. Puppet shows are very popular in Myanmar and often last for hours, sometimes all night long.

Fascinating as the puppets were, I found myself pulled towards the kitchen, where I found Harriot cooking. Her kitchen reflected their relative prosperity, with a stove and refrigerator. It was cool and dark, tucked into the shady side of the house. I watched fascinated as Harriot stuffed rice balls with fried soy beans and garlic, smothered them with fresh tomato sauce and then crumbled roasted peanuts on top. She also lightly fried chicken balls spiced with salt, garlic, chillies and coriander and then placed them on top of fresh warm green mustard leaves. As she cooked, she explained to me that the Shan are very fond of spicy food, relied on fresh locally grown ingredients, and that rice and soy bean powder (*tua naw kep*) are their staples.

Lunch was served on the front porch and I gobbled it up. The chicken balls were scrumptious, crispy brown on the outside, tender, juicy and spicy on the inside, all of it enhanced by the sourness of the green mustard leaves. The dish was surprisingly light, although the hotness of the chillies lingered on the palate. The rice salad was refreshing, as the tomatoes were bursting with flavour and the peanuts added a rich crunch.

Harriot and I quickly became fast friends and I spent many a pleasant afternoon hanging around her kitchen. She introduced me to Sai Khin Maung, a dashing young university student who became my Shan translator, accompanying me on many of my travels in the Shan state. Sai Khin was from Mogok, a town in the northern Shan state known for its ruby mines. He spoke good English, as well as Shan and Burmese. The Shan language, which is closely related to Thai and Lao, has managed to maintain its integrity, although most Shan are also fluent in Burmese and few read and write Shan. It's a very melodic language, and I found it relaxing to listen to Sai Khin as he discussed recipes in the marketplace and in restaurants. He painstakingly translated each recipe for me, and sampled all sorts of foods even he had never tried.

Our first excursion into the Shan state was to Inle Lake, the second largest natural lake in Myanmar. It is home to the Intha people who live in towns around the lake and on the lake itself in floating villages, where they tend very productive floating vegetable gardens and even worship at floating temples. The Intha, who are Tibeto-Burman in origin, speak an archaic dialect of Burmese. Perhaps the most unusual thing about them is their practice of leg rowing. Because parts of the lake are covered with reeds and other floating plants, it is often difficult to navigate from a seated position. So the men stand at the stern balanced on one leg, with the other leg wrapped around an oar, the foot on the flat of the oar. They then row by pressing down with their feet. Inle Lake is also home to the world's only jumping cat monastery, where the monks teach stray cats to jump through small hoops. I never quite understood the religious significance, but it was pretty amazing to watch.

Sai Khin and I stayed in a charming guesthouse and restaurant on the lake, called the Four Sisters Inn. One evening, I sat in the kitchen and watched four older women (I think they were the sisters) prepare *htamin gyin*, which is squeezed rice with fish. They were pleased and excited to have an eager audience as they kneaded fresh carp, tomatoes and chillies into rice, then cooked the mixture and shaped it into balls that they seasoned with soy bean powder, shallots, garlic and coriander. The result was delicious, piquant and densely flavourful. The inn had the unusual practice of having dinner guests decide how much they wanted to pay for their meals. I think it is quite a clever policy because we paid more than they probably would have charged.

Sai Khin and I quickly developed a routine in our travels. We would arrive in a town, find a nice guesthouse and rest early so that we could rise early for the *kaat* or marketplace. I had been told that the *kaats* would be the best place to get a sense of Shan cuisine, and to experience it at the stands selling prepared food. These markets begin early, often before dawn, and are held five days a week in virtually every village, town and city in the Shan state. And so Sai Khin and I would set off at first light, armed with pens, notebooks, cameras and a dictionary. I quickly learned that the markets, like so much in Myanmar, are raucous studies in barely controlled chaos. It took me a while to develop the confidence and skills needed to navigate through the myriad shoppers and aggressive vendors, who are mostly women, and sell everything from aubergines to *longyis* to machine parts. The moment they see you even glance at one of their tomatoes, it is yours! My advice to a market novice is to wear sunglasses! You will save a lot of money and avoid ending up with 100 tomatoes! And if you buy from someone two days in a row, she will remember you and heckle you if you choose to buy a tomato from her neighbour. Trust me, I learned this the hard way. But once you find your way around, life in the marketplace becomes a wonderful adventure.

All kinds of people visit the market, but it is mostly women who rise early to get the freshest food for the day's meals, refrigerators being a rarity in Myanmar. It is a common sight to see a woman with a small child strapped to her back in a sling, carrying a big basket for her shopping. When finished, they either strap the baskets onto their bicycles or balance them on top of their heads and pedal home. I have also seen Shan with firewood, live chickens, everything but the kitchen sink, strapped onto their bikes—and still have room for the whole family. The people of Myanmar have an amazing sense of balance—it is truly astonishing how much they can get onto one bicycle and still ride it! A friend of mine swears she once saw someone transporting a refrigerator on his bicycle!

Whichever town or village Sai Khin and I visited, the marketplace was my favourite stop. I found real joy browsing through the beautiful displays of vibrant and colourful freshly-picked fruit and vegetables, ginger, garlic, shallots, coriander, galangal (a root that looks a bit like ginger, but has a slightly sweet taste), potatoes, ladies fingers, spices I have never seen or heard of, bamboo shoot, cuttlefish, eel and fresh prawns. Fish was often hard to find in the Shan state, especially saltwater fish, so it was a major treat and often sold out quickly. I saw more varieties of rice than I knew existed, including long, short, medium, white, wild and basmati, some far more expensive than others. I also learnt that the kind of rice one buys is an indicator of social class and status. Then there were Shan delicacies such as ant eggs called *mot som* (sour ant), crickets, cicadas, frogs, wasp larvae and *ii kook* (the embryo of the scarab beetle). And of course, you could also complete your wardrobe and furnish your house at the market.

The markets gave me a real sense of the Shan people, who are friendly, lively, humorous and handsome, with wide features, large eyes, round mouths and beautiful jet-black hair that the woman wear long. They love to cook highly aromatic dishes. They also love to wear brightly-coloured clothes, in fact they love colour in general, painting their bicycles and store fronts vibrant hues. The markets were my classroom and I was an eager pupil; on more than one occasion, I tried the patience of my teachers with my endless questions.

My favourite place at the market was invariably the food stalls, where I could watch the vendors cook, learn about Shan ingredients, acquire recipes and satisfy my American longing for instant gratification in a most delicious way. I discovered many wonderful dishes at the stalls. There was Shan noodle soup—a hearty broth with noodles and succulent chicken or pork that is first marinated in a tangy tomato sauce infused with garlic, ginger and shallots. The soup is garnished before serving with crushed, roasted peanuts and fresh coriander. I also loved steamed fish—succulent fresh fish seasoned with ginger, mint, garlic, coriander and a touch of fish sauce. Wrapped in banana leaf and steamed, the fish is then served on a bed of basmati rice. The Shan have a sweet tooth and I happily discovered *tamin*— glutinous steamed rice sweetened with sugar and coconut milk, wrapped in banana leaf and then warmed in the oven or over a fire. Another favourite sweet was *khao tom glauy* (steamed bananas in sticky rice). Grazing happily through the markets, my palate was awakened—and so was my sense of wonder.

Over the following seven months, I made over a dozen trips through the Shan state, usually accompanied by Sai Khin, and always returning to my base

A typical morning market scene in Lashio Lay, where the locals
arrive early to jostle for the best and freshest produce.

Throughout the Shan state, fresh produce is brought to the markets where the sellers and buyers engage in lively banter. Clockwise from top left: A man with a traditional Shan bag draped across his shoulders sells wheat at a roadside market in Yangon; an elderly lady sells freshly-cut flowers in Taunggyi; while a Shan man sells vegetables in Hsipaw.

The colourful array of food and goods sold at the morning markets. Clockwise from top left: Nuts, grains and spices stored in colourful *longyis*; stacks of dried fermented soy bean cakes (*tau naw kep*) are tied with twine; stacks of wooden clogs worn mainly in the rainy season; and gourds, a favourite in Myanmar, are often found in many shapes and sizes.

Shan restaurants are a great place to grab a quick bite throughout the day. Clockwise from top left: A lady preparing rice noodles at a roadside stall in Yangon; a young girl preparing vegetables at a morning market; a Shan restaurant located right in the middle of a strawberry field in Pyin U Lwin (They are known not only for their tasty food, but also for the best strawberry juice in all of Myanmar.); and rice noodles being prepared at various street stalls.

Cooking over an open fire is fairly typical in Myanmar, especially in the hill towns and villages. Anti-clockwise from top: An elderly lady grills fish wrapped in banana leaf (*pa mok*) over a charcoal fire; a cast iron wok set over a stone stove; and a large bamboo steamer is set over a pot of water placed over an open flame. These steamers are used for steaming meats, fish, vegetables and tofu.

Typical tools of the trade. Above: Stone mortar and pestles are widely used in Myanmar for grinding herbs, spices and grains. Right: cleavers are a handy tool for cutting meats and vegetables. This lady is cutting chicken with a cleaver at a morning market in Mandalay.

in wonderful Mandalay. My preferred mode of travel was the bus. I preferred it because it was my only choice. Bus travel in Myanmar makes train travel seem like first class on Singapore Airlines. Since most of the roads are not paved, getting to places can take a long time. And since the bus as a means of transportation is cheap, everybody takes it! The sheer intensity of the experience is mitigated by the bus boys who basically run the show. They not only help the driver navigate the narrow, harrowing roads at speeds that made my belly do belly flops, they herd—and sometimes squeeze—everyone on and off the bus, and take care of the luggage. I found them charming and solicitous of foreign women. They often found me a decent seat and made sure that no one hassled me. I developed an enormous respect and affection for them. They would play great Burmese music tapes and sing at the top of their lungs as they hung out of the bus with their *longyis* blowing in the wind. They came from all over Myanmar and on their days off, many stayed at welcoming monasteries. I became friends with one bus boy and he bought me jasmine flowers for my hair and rode me around on the back of his bicycle, showing me the sights of Mandalay. It was one of the highlights of my stay in Myanmar!

Sai Khin and I had a heavenly trip to Maymo, a town in the cool foothills east of Mandalay. A prosperous trading town and hill station for centuries, Maymo is filled with an eclectic mix of Shan, British colonial and Chinese architecture. Brightly-painted pony-drawn wagons are everywhere and the town is known for growing strawberries, flowers and European fruit and vegetables, all of which flourish in the cool climate. Sai Khin and I had a delicious meal at a quaint outdoor restaurant—also brightly painted—that was nestled among strawberry fields. It was here that I tried my first Shan tomato salad; a refreshing and spicy blend of fresh tomatoes, fried shallots, garlic, green chillies, white vinegar and toasted sesame seeds, topped off with fresh coriander. It came with a bowl of rice and a tall glass of ice-cold strawberry juice. A dream lunch!

One of my most memorable market experiences was in Kyauk Mei, a village near the city of Hsipaw in the Shan state. I was on my last leg after a long morning and needed some sustenance. I plopped down on a stool at a noodle stall, placed my order and watched as a charming Shan woman, her jet-black hair pulled back into a tight bun, prepared my noodle soup. I was mesmerized by her rhythm and deft movements. It was like watching a symphony conductor. With confidence, economy and grace, she cut up fresh tomatoes and tossed them into the clear, simmering broth. She then chopped shallots and into the pot they went, followed by a dollop of coriander and then the noodles. Finally, she drizzled in sweet soy sauce. The result was fragrant, flavourful and hardy, slightly sweet, slightly spicy and completely nourishing to the body and soul.

Hsipaw itself is a fascinating place. The Sawbwas, feudal rulers of Hsipaw, lived for centuries in a palace at the northern end of the town. The last Sawbwa lord disappeared during the military coup in 1962, and when I visited the palace, I found it cared for by his nephew, Donald, and Donald's wife, Fern. They were eager for company and told me endless stories about what their family went through. They also gave me a wonderful recipe for ginger chicken, slowly cooked in a clay pot until it is tender and juicy. Not long after my visit, Donald was jailed for his political activism, and as far as I know, he remains in prison.

The central market at Hsipaw is one of the best markets in Myanmar. Shans, Kachins and other tribes come to trade, so the mix is lively indeed. You have to go early—the market starts at 3:30 a.m. and is pretty much wrapped up by 6:00 a.m. One morning, I came across a young man making what looked like a fascinating dish. First, he put cooked potatoes, red chillies, shallots, garlic, spinach and tomatoes into a wok and cooked them over high heat, then he poured the mixture over rice and wrapped it all in a banana leaf that he steamed in a covered wooden steamer. When I unwrapped the banana leaf, I was first hit by the bold aroma of the chillies, followed by the slightly more mellow garlic, and finally a whiff of the banana leaf. The flavour was out of this world! The Shan eat this and many other dishes with their fingers, believing that it adds flavour to the food; I opted for chopsticks. I photographed each step of the preparation of this dish and showed the pictures to Sai Khin, who explained that it was a vegetable *mok* (Potato and Rice Steamed in Banana Leaves, page 132).

After each excursion into the Shan State, I would return to the comfort of my Mandalay guest house, hang out with my friends, old and new, get my photographs printed, and work on my newest recipes, often with Sai Khin's invaluable help. The months passed quickly. One day, I realised I had fallen in love with the Shan people and their cuisine.

This cookbook is reflection of that love.

Eating with the Shan

Eating a meal with a Shan family is a joy. They love food and treat meals at home as an opportunity to show that respect.

Of course, they also love their equivalent of fast food, served from carts or trucks, but even this is prepared with a certain reverence and grace, although it is often eaten with ravenous speed.

I treasured my invitations to Shan households. Most homes have a dining room with a low table. Everyone sits on the floor and all the different dishes are placed at the centre of the table, within easy reach of each person at the table. There are no courses except dessert. A typical meal consists of steamed rice, a meat or fish dish, vegetables, salad, soup, tofu, and an array of spicy dipping sauces and condiments such as chilli oil, bird's eye chillies, coriander and dark and light soy sauce. The Shan have a 'sour tooth' and there will almost always be a side of pickled vegetables or mustard. Sticky rice is rolled into a ball and used to soak up sauces and curries, never bread. Alcohol is rarely served, but green tea is ubiquitous, both at meal times and throughout the day.

Rather than passing dishes around the table, those at the table will reach to the centre for what they want, help themselves, then put the dish back. There was never any grabbing or rushing—well, maybe occasionally when there was a teenager around. Of course, being a guest, I was treated with a certain deference and everyone was on their best behaviour!

The Shan eat with their fingertips, believing it enhances the flavour of the food, the exception being noodles where chopsticks are used. At first, I found this practice a bit off-putting, being a germ-sensitive Western gal, and I often opted for chopsticks. As time wore on, however, I used them less and less. Soup is served in small bowls and sipped like tea throughout the meal.

A Shan meal is about the food and unlike many Western cultures, there is no great premium placed on lively conversation. In the villages and rural areas, the women in the family stay in the kitchen and do not sit at the table during the meal, with the exception of the grandmother or any other elderly lady who is present. (A household is typically made up of three generations living together.) Dinner, especially, can be quite a crowded affair, with the immediate family, relatives and invited neighbours and guests, present at the table.

Food is plentiful at mealtimes, but not overwhelming. After everyone has eaten and the table cleared, fresh fruit and dessert are brought out. The Shan adore mangoes in particular—and if ever there was a food designed to be eaten with the fingers, it is a stringy, juicy mango! Popular desserts include *suay tamin*, sticky rice balls covered with brown sugar, then dipped in coconut milk and grilled; and *nya bin kau ni*, sticky rice with sugar and bananas wrapped in a banana leaf and then put in the oven or on the grill.

The Shan eat three main meals a day, with breakfast usually being small and simple. Some popular breakfast dishes are *to hpu nway*, warm tofu with rice noodles, and *khou pooke*, sticky rice cake mixed with sesame seeds and honey. Lunch for the working crowd is often from roadside stands or carts, or eaten at tiny restaurants that spill out into the streets.

I felt very privileged to enjoy meals with Shan families. Their warmth and hospitality complemented the delicious food and always left me content in both body and soul.

In writing this cookbook, I have taken into account the difficulty of obtaining certain ingredients outside of Myanmar and the availability of modern kitchen conveniences such as blenders and ovens in modern homes. I have thus modified the recipes using ingredients that are readily available, but which offer a similar taste and flavour, and included the use of modern kitchen conveniences for quicker preparation and cooking times. Enjoy!

Sauces and Dips

Shan meals are always served with sauces and dips, and these same sauces and dips also accompany snacks such as Shan rolls, fried tofu and raw vegetables—which the Shan love—to give them an extra kick. One of my favourite things to do is to pour these sauces over rice or rice noodles for a quick but tasty meal.

Aubergine Dip
Ka Yan Thee Nat

I got this recipe from Sai Khin Maung, a charming young man who served as my guide and translator on one of my trips to Myanmar. Sai Khin lived in Mandalay, but was a native of Mogok, a ruby mining town in northern Shan state.

YIELDS 2 CUPS

2 aubergines (eggplants), about 625 g (1 lb 5^1/$_2$ oz)

2 cloves garlic, peeled and finely chopped

2 bird's eye chillies, seeded and minced

1 shallot, peeled and finely chopped

2 tsp fish sauce or light soy sauce

^{1}/$_2$ tsp salt

Preheat oven to 210°C (410°F).

Rinse aubergines and pat dry. Pierce aubergines on all sides with a fork.

Line a baking tray with parchment paper or aluminium foil.
Place aubergines on tray and bake for 40 minutes or until soft.
Set aside to cool.

Peel aubergines and finely chop. Place in a bowl.

Add garlic, chillies, shallot, fish sauce or light soy sauce and salt to bowl and mix well. Adjust seasoning to taste if necessary.

Enjoy as a dip with vegetable sticks or crackers.

Mango Salsa
Tha Yet Thee Pan Twe

Mango salsa is the perfect solution for "cooling down" the tongue when eating spicy food. The combination of sweetness from the sugar and tartness from the mango, temper the intensity of the spice. The Shan enjoy mango salsa with fish and meat, or on its own.

YIELDS 2 CUPS

1 green (unripe) mango, peeled and shredded

1 bird's eye chilli, seeded and minced

$1/2$ red onion, peeled and finely chopped

$1/4$ cup coriander leaves (cilantro), finely chopped

1 tsp sugar

1 Tbsp freshly squeezed lime juice

Salt to taste

Place mango, chilli, onion, coriander leaves, sugar, lime juice and salt in a bowl. Mix well.

Serve and enjoy at room temperature.

Vinegar and Sesame Dip
Sha La Ka Yae Nan

Vinegar and sesame dip is generally served when eating fried foods such as Shan rolls or fried tofu. The myriad flavors of garlic, vinegar, ginger and sesame make this a dip a favorite with the Shan people because it is easy to make and tastes delicious.

YIELDS 1 CUP

1/2 cup white wine vinegar

1/4 cup rice wine vinegar

1 Tbsp + 1 tsp sugar

2 cloves garlic, peeled and finely chopped

2 bird's eye chillies, seeded and minced

2.5-cm (1-in) knob ginger, peeled and grated

1/4 cup coriander leaves (cilantro), finely chopped

1 shallot, peeled and finely chopped

1 Tbsp white sesame seeds, toasted

1/2 tsp salt

1 Tbsp + 1 tsp sesame oil

Put vinegars and sugar in a frying pan over low heat. Cook stirring until sugar dissolves. Pour into a bowl.

Add add remaining ingredients to bowl and stir to mix.

Serve with Shan Rolls (page 127), Twice-fried Tofu Fritters (page 105) or other fried foods.

NOTE: Toasting nuts enhances their nutty flavour and gives them a firm texture. The same is true for sesame seeds. To toast these tiny seeds, place them in a frying pan and heat them until they just start to turn brown and you can smell a nutty aroma. Once they reach that point—it only takes a few minutes—remove them immediately from the heat and pour onto a plate or flat surface and run a wooden spoon over the top to spread them out. Let the toasted seeds cool before adding to your recipe. To store, keep in an airtight container

Pounded Roasted Tomatoes

Nampit Mak Ker Some

The Shan season their food with fermented soy beans (*hto nao*). This is very difficult to find outside Myanmar, so I have used dried black beans which have a similar flavour. Alternatively, use fish sauce.

YIELDS 4 CUPS

Salt to taste

3 large whole tomatoes, cores removed

2–3 Tbsp black beans or 3 tsp fish sauce

4 cloves garlic, peeled and finely chopped

3 bird's eye chillies, seeded and minced

1 stalk celery, cleaned and finely chopped

1/2 cup coriander leaves (cilantro), finely chopped

Bring a large pot of water to the boil. Add in 1 tsp salt, then add tomatoes and blanch for about 1 minute. Remove tomatoes and place in a bowl of cool water.

Prepare dried black beans, if using. Place a frying pan over medium-high heat. Add black beans and toast for about 2 minutes, stirring frequently so beans do not burn. Remove from heat and allow to cool. Place cooled beans in a mortar and grind until powdery. If black beans are not available, omit this step and use fish sauce as a substitute.

Drain tomatoes and peel off skins. Slice in half and cut into 0.5-cm (1/4-in) cubes.

Place tomatoes with remaining ingredients in a mixing bowl. Mix well for about 5 minutes.

This is perfect with fresh vegetables such as cabbage, string beans or cucumbers.

Tamarind Sauce
Man Jee Thee Pwe

Tamarind is by nature sour, but when mixed with sugar, chillies and fish sauce, it takes on a rich flavour that is wonderful with various fish (especially prawns) and certain fried foods such as Shan rolls.

YIELDS 1 CUP

10 tamarind pods or 1 Tbsp tamarind pulp

2 cloves garlic, peeled and finely chopped

4 bird's eye chillies, seeded and minced

2 Tbsp finely chopped coriander leaves (cilantro)

2 tsp sugar

1 Tbsp fish sauce

Salt to taste

Prepare tamarind liquid. If using tamarind pods, peel pods and remove fibres. Bring a small pot of water to the boil, then remove from heat. Add tamarind and leave to steep for 15–20 minutes. Reserve 1/2 cup liquid with the tamarind and discard the rest. Use fingers to mash tamarind pulp into the liquid, then strain. Discard seeds and fibre.

If using tamarind pulp, soak it in 1/2 cup warm water for about 10 minutes, then mash with a spoon or hands to dissolve the tamarind. Strain liquid and discard seeds and fibre.

Using a mortar and pestle or blender, mix tamarind liquid with all remaining ingredients. The sauce should be pasty.

Serve with fish dishes or Shan Rolls (page 127).

Spicy Pork Dip

Nam Pid Aung

This dip is a meal in itself. It is traditionally eaten with raw vegetables and deep-fried pork rind, but it also goes well with sticky rice. This is quite a treat!

YIELDS 4 CUPS

1 Tbsp dried prawn (shrimp) paste

2 garlic cloves, peeled and finely chopped

2 shallots, peeled and finely chopped

3 dried chillies or 1–2 bird's eye chillies, minced

220 g (8 oz) minced pork

2 ripe tomatoes, finely chopped

1/4 cup canola oil

1/4 cup chicken stock (page 44)

1 tsp salt

1¹/₂ Tbsp sugar

Combine prawn paste, garlic, shallots, chillies, minced pork and tomatoes in a bowl and mix well.

Heat oil in a frying pan over medium heat. Add pork mixture, chicken stock, salt and sugar. Stir well and bring to a simmer. Cook for about 20 minutes until tomatoes are soft. Remove from heat and allow to cool.

Serve the sauce as is or process in a blender for a smooth consistency.

Adjust seasoning to taste and serve.

Serve with raw vegetables, deep-fried pork rind or sticky rice.

Soups

A Shan meal is never complete without a soup or broth. The soup stays on the table throughout the entire meal, often in a large bowl placed at the centre of the table, from which diners serve themselves as desired. The soup is used to cleanse the palate between dishes, and to cool off the tongue if a dish is too spicy for one's taste.

Shan Chicken Soup 44

Chicken Soup with Bamboo Shoot
in Coconut Milk 46

Dried Mustard Soup 48

Mustard Soup *Phact Saw* 49

Watercress Soup 51

Mango Soup 52

Shan Chicken Soup

This truly is chicken soup for the soul. My Shan friends prefer the soup with less chicken, but I say the more chicken the better! Serve on its own or with white rice.

SERVES 6

1 Tbsp vegetable oil

6 cloves garlic, peeled and thinly sliced

5-cm (2-in) ginger, peeled and grated

1 tsp salt

$^1/_2$ tsp ground black pepper

$^1/_2$ cup coriander leaves (cilantro), chopped

A few sprigs mint, thinly sliced

Chicken Stock

2 kg (4$^1/_2$ lb) whole chicken

1 carrot, chopped

2 stalks celery, chopped

1 medium yellow onion, peeled and cut into quarters

2.5-cm (1-in) knob ginger, peeled and thinly sliced

1 Tbsp finely chopped coriander leaves (cilantro)

Enough water to cover chicken

1 tsp salt

$^1/_4$ tsp ground black pepper

Start by preparing chicken stock. In large, deep pot, add chicken, carrot, celery, onion, ginger and coriander. Add enough water to cover chicken, then season with salt and pepper. Bring to the boil, lower heat and simmer for about 1$^1/_2$ hours.

Remove chicken from stock and allow to cool. Strain stock. Shred chicken meat and discard skin and bones.

To prepare the soup, heat the oil, garlic, ginger, salt and pepper in a large pot over medium heat. Reduce heat to low, then cover pot and cook for about 5 minutes. Remove lid and add 10 cups chicken stock. Bring to the boil and add shredded chicken. Reduce heat and simmer for 45 minutes.

Add coriander and mint to soup and continue to cook for another 15 minutes. Adjust to taste with salt and pepper.

Serve hot or at room temperature.

NOTE: The shredded chicken and stock can be prepared in advance. Pack separately and store refrigerated.

Chicken Soup with Bamboo Shoot and Coconut Milk

I got this recipe from a Shan professor teaching in Chiang Mai, Thailand. I was skeptical that it was an authentic Shan dish, as it tasted more Thai than Shan. However, she reassured me that this is indeed a Shan recipe. This soup is very popular in the northern Shan state and it has quickly become a favourite among my friends here in the US as well!

SERVES 4

1 Tbsp vegetable oil

1 Tbsp chilli flakes, or to taste

900 g (2 lb) boneless chicken, chopped into 2.5-cm (1-in) pieces

390 g (14 oz) can coconut milk

3 cups chicken stock (page 44)

2 cans bamboo shoots, each 220 g (8 oz), drained and sliced

1 large aubergine (eggplant), cut into 5-cm (2-in) pieces

450 g (1 lb) green beans, ends trimmed

Salt to taste

¹/₂ Tbsp crisp-fried shallots

Heat oil in a 5-litre (8-pint) casserole dish over medium-low heat. Add chilli flakes and cook for about 2 minutes, stirring constantly, being careful not to let chilli flakes burn.

Add chicken and brown on all sides, but do not cook through. Gradually add coconut milk and simmer for about 6 minutes.

Add chicken stock, bamboo shoots, aubergine, green beans and salt to taste. Simmer, uncovered, for 2 hours.

Garnish with crisp-fried shallots and serve hot.

Dried Mustard Soup

I love dried mustard leaves, so this soup is my idea of liquid heaven. It's a perfect way to cleanse the palate while eating spicy food—a few sips in between bites is a popular Shan way to enjoy this soup. Or, do like I do and pour it in a mug and drink it like tea. Dried mustard leaves are very tasty and tangy, and if you've never tried it, this is the perfect opportunity.

SERVES 2

3 cups water

2 cups dried mustard leaves, rinsed and chopped

1 clove garlic, peeled and finely chopped

2.5-cm (1-in) ginger, peeled and thinly sliced

1 bird's eye chilli, minced

Salt to taste

Bring water to the boil, then remove from heat.

Place dried mustard leaves, garlic, ginger and chillies into 2 bowls. Adjust the amounts according to taste. Season with salt.

Pour hot water into bowls and serve at room temperature.

Mustard Soup
Phact Saw

I got this recipe from my Shan friend, Harriot, who claims that she makes the best mustard soup in all of Mandalay! After trying it, I hope you'll agree. Being a mustard aficionado, I loved the way it made Harriot's kitchen smell. This is the Shan's favourite soup and it's very easy to make. It's a triple treat—fast, healthy and fabulous!

SERVES 4

**1 bunch fresh mustard greens, rinsed
   and base trimmed**

1 Tbsp vegetable oil

1 shallot, peeled and finely chopped

3 cloves garlic, peeled and finely chopped

2.5-cm (1-in) ginger, peeled and thinly sliced

1 tsp tamarind pulp

4 tomatoes, finely chopped

8 cups vegetable stock

Salt to taste

Bring a pot of water to the boil. Add 1 tsp salt, then add mustard greens and blanch for about 1 minute. Drain mustard greens and leave to cool before chopping finely.

Heat oil in a casserole dish over medium heat. Add shallot, garlic and ginger. Cook, stirring, until shallots are tender. Takes about 5 minutes.

Stir in tamarind pulp, then tomatoes and mustard greens. Cook for another 10 minutes.

Add stock and bring to the boil. Reduce heat to a simmer and cook, uncovered, for about 1 hour until soup thickens slightly.

Season to taste with salt. Serve hot.

NOTE: Blanching the mustard greens before cooking helps to preserve their colour and tones down the bitter taste.

Watercress Soup

Watercress is a popular ingredient in Shan curries. Not only is watercress extremely nutritious and tasty, some people believe it is an aphrodisiac. This watercress soup is one of my favourites, refreshing with an intriguing mix of flavours and textures. As for it being an aphrodisiac, well, try it and see!

SERVES 6

2 Tbsp vegetable oil

1 medium yellow onion, peeled and finely chopped

8 cloves garlic, peeled and thinly sliced

2 medium tomatoes, seeds removed and cut into 1-cm (1/2-in) cubes

1 tsp salt

1/2 tsp ground black pepper

4 cups chicken stock (page 44)

2 bunches watercress, cleaned, stems removed and chopped

1/2 lime, grated for zest and juice extracted

Heat oil in a large pot over medium heat. Add onion, garlic, tomatoes, salt and pepper. Reduce heat to low, cover and cook for 15 minutes, stirring occasionally.

Remove lid and add chicken stock. Bring to the boil, then reduce to a simmer and add watercress.

Simmer for another 5 minutes, then remove from heat. Stir in lime zest and juice and adjust seasoning if necessary. Serve immediately.

Mango Soup

Mango is said to neutralise stomach acidity, so this soup is great to sip when you're eating spicy curries. Not only does this soup taste delicious, it is also a breeze to make.

SERVES 2

2 cups water

2 dried whole mangoes, cut into strips

1 clove garlic, peeled and thinly sliced

**2.5-cm (1-in) knob ginger, peeled and
thinly sliced**

**2 Tbsp coriander leaves (cilantro),
finely chopped**

Salt to taste

Bring water to the boil, then remove from heat.

Divide mangoes, garlic, ginger and coriander between 2 bowls. Add salt to taste. Pour hot water into bowls and let it sit until the mangoes soften. Takes about 3 minutes.

Serve and enjoy!

NOTE: Whole, dried mangoes are available from some supermarkets with a well-stocked dried food and nuts section.

Salads

Salads (*thout*) are served as part of a Shan meal, but they can be eaten on their own with a bowl of rice. The portion size is small and, like soup, salads are often used to cleanse the palate during the meal. Sometimes, instead of a salad, plates of raw fresh vegetables will be set out on the table for nibbling throughout the meal.

Shan Tomato Salad *Pan Twe Pwe Thot* 56

Mango Salad *Tha Yet Thee Thot* 59

Mushroom Salad 61

Vermicelli Salad *Jar Zan Thot* 62

Shan Tomato Salad
Pan Twe Pwe Thot

This is another recipe from Harriot. She is a great cook and loves to entertain and talk about books and food. I met her through my friend, Emma, and we became frequent dinner guests at her welcoming home, where we not only learned how to cook traditional Shan food, but also the art of Shan puppetry. This salad is one of my favourites, especially when served with hot rice. I just love to smother the rice with the salad and eat it with a cup of hot Shan tea!

SERVES 4

3 Tbsp vegetable oil

2 cloves garlic, peeled and thinly sliced

1 shallot, peeled and finely chopped

4 medium tomatoes, sliced

2–3 bird's eye chillies, thinly sliced

1 red onion, peeled and thinly sliced

3 tsp fish sauce

1 tsp sugar

2–3 Tbsp white rice vinegar

1 Tbsp white sesame seeds, toasted

2 Tbsp finely chopped coriander leaves (cilantro)

Salt and pepper to taste

Heat oil in a frying pan over medium heat. Add garlic and shallot and fry until golden brown and crisp. Takes 3–4 minutes. Be careful not to burn garlic, or it will be bitter.

Strain oil and reserve. Place browned garlic and shallots on a paper towel to absorb excess oil. Pat dry.

Put sliced tomatoes in a medium bowl.

Mix the oil, chillies, red onion, fish sauce, sugar, white rice vinegar, sesame seeds, garlic, shallots and coriander together in a small bowl.

Pour mixture over tomatoes and toss gently. I find this is best done with your hands. Taste and adjust seasoning if necessary.

Serve and enjoy!

NOTE: Scrape out the seeds of the chillies for less intense heat and keep them in for more heat. Always wash hands after working with chilies, or wear gloves, as the oils in chillies can leave a burning sensation on skin.

Mango Salad
Tha yet thee thot

Mango salad makes a wonderful addition to any spicy meal. This refreshing salad has a perfect balance of flavours and compliments any meat or fish curry. If you are craving sweet and sour, this is your dish!

SERVES 2

1 green (unripe) mango, peeled and finely grated

1 shallot, peeled and thinly sliced

1–2 bird's eye chillies, minced

1 tsp sugar

1 tsp white rice vinegar (optional)

Salt to taste

Combine all ingredients and mix well.

Enjoy with spicy curries or white rice.

Mushroom Salad

One day, I went into a seamstress's shop in Mandalay to get some clothes altered. It turned out the seamstress was Shan. When I told her I was working on a cookbook, she volunteered to share some family recipes including this one. But once she got going about her repertoire, I thought I would be stuck there for days! The Shan not only love to cook, they love to talk. (Fortunately they are almost invariably charming and helpful.) If you like mushrooms, this a great side at any meal, and equally wonderful on its own.

SERVES 4–6

**280 g (10 oz) button mushrooms,
  wiped cleaned**

**2 spring onions (scallions), ends trimmed
  and thinly sliced**

2 Tbsp chopped coriander leaves (cilantro)

1–2 bird's eye chillies, minced

**2 Tbsp cilantro (coriander) (Chinese parsley),
  finely chopped**

1 tsp sugar or liquid jaggery (palm sugar)

2 Tbsp lemon juice or white rice vinegar

Salt to taste

Steam mushrooms until just tender. Takes about 20 minutes.
Place in a medium bowl and let cool.

Add remaining ingredients and mix well.

Serve and enjoy!

NOTE: Button mushrooms often have specks of dirt on them. To clean,
do not wash—they will absorb water and turn soft and mushy. Gently wipe
the dirt away with a clean towel.

Vermicelli Salad
Jar Zan Thot

Vermicelli is ubiquitous throughout Myanmar and for good reason!
It tastes great no matter what you do with it! Vermicelli salad is no
exception. This is a light salad that is sure to hit the spot! You can also
make this salad more substantial by adding grilled chicken or pork.

SERVES 4

Salt to taste

450 g (1 lb) dried rice vermicelli

2–3 Tbsp white rice vinegar

1 Tbsp lime juice

1 tsp sugar

3 Tbsp finely chopped coriander leaves (cilantro)

1 Tbsp white sesame seeds, toasted

4 Tbsp roasted peanuts, crushed

Bring a large pot of water to the boil. Add 1 tsp salt and turn off heat.
Add vermicelli and stir gently. Leave to soak for 10–15 minutes until
tender. Drain and put in a medium bowl.

Mix together rice vinegar, lime juice and sugar in a small bowl. Taste and
adjust with salt. Stir in coriander leaves and sesame seeds.

Pour mixture over vermicelli and mix well. Top with peanuts and serve.

NOTE: Crushed peanuts add a wonderful nutty flavour and texture to many
Shan dishes. To make them, start with raw or unsalted roasted peanuts. Do not
use flavoured or salted nuts, as these will impart flavours into your dish that
you don't want. Lay out a single layer of peanuts on a flat surface and cover with
parchment paper. Using a heavy rolling pin or a heavy can, roll firmly over the
peanuts until you get the desired texture.

Fish and Seafood

Because the Shan state is landlocked, seafood is often hard to find and considered a great treat. This is a marked contrast to the rest of Myanmar, where seafood is a staple. When they're available in the Shan state, prawns and crab are popular food choices. The region around Inle Lake is the best place to get freshwater fish, especially carp, which is usually wrapped in banana leaves, then baked or steamed.

Fried Inle Fish

This fried fish is popular in the Inle Lake region in Shan state. It is nicknamed the "sufferin' fish" as the process of preparing the fish involves skinning, deboning and pounding. The pounded flesh is then stuffed back into the skin and deep-fried. It is a delicious dish and a must-try if in Myanmar. I have tweaked the recipe to omit skinning and deboning the fish, as it can be tricky and labour intensive.

SERVES 4

1 whole fish such as pike or carp, about 1.3 kg (3 lb), cleaned

2 Tbsp light soy sauce

1 tsp ground turmeric

Salt and pepper to taste

$^1/_2$ cup plain (all-purpose) flour

2–4 cups vegetable oil

Stuffing

150 g (5$^1/_3$ oz) fish roe or $^1/_2$ cup fresh bread crumbs

1 egg, if using bread crumbs

2 Tbsp coriander leaves (cilantro)

1-cm ($^1/_2$-in) knob ginger, peeled and finely chopped

2 cloves garlic, peeled and finely chopped

1 shallot, peeled and finely chopped

$^1/_2$ lime, grated for zest

2 bird's eye chillies, minced

Sauce

2 Tbsp finely chopped coriander leaves (cilantro)

2 cloves garlic, peeled and finely chopped

1 shallot, peeled and finely chopped

1-cm ($^1/_2$-in) knob ginger, peeled and shredded

$^1/_2$ lime, grated for zest

1 Tbsp toasted black bean powder (page 39)

1 cup chicken stock (page 44)

2 Tbsp thick dark soy sauce

1 lime, juice extracted

Combine all stuffing ingredients in bowl and mix well.

Rub the inside and outside of fish with soy sauce, turmeric, salt and pepper. Place stuffing into cavity of fish and secure with toothpicks or kitchen twine to prevent the stuffing from falling out while frying. Pat fish dry with paper towels and dust with flour.

In a heavy frying pan over medium-high heat, add oil so it is about 2.5-cm (1-in) deep. Heat, then carefully lower fish into pan and fry for about 5 minutes on each side until golden brown. Drain and remove fish.

Drain oil from pan, then add ingredients for sauce. Return fish to pan and cover. Braise fish over medium-low heat for 15–20 minutes or until cooked through.

Remove fish and place on serving platter. Continue simmering the sauce until reduced by half. Season with salt and pepper and pour over fish.

Serve hot with white rice.

Stir-fried Fish with Soy Beans

Salted soy beans are definitely an acquired taste, but well worth the try. I grew to love this dish, another that my friend, Sai Aung Tun, first prepared for me. The combination of soy beans and tomatoes stir-fried with ginger and coriander leaves is to die for!

SERVES 2

2 tilapia fillets, each about 150 g (5^1/$_3$ oz) cleaned and pat dry

2 Tbsp vegetable oil

1 shallot, peeled and thinly sliced

1 Tbsp grated ginger

2 whole tomatoes, finely chopped

A pinch of sugar

1 Tbsp salted soy beans

1 Tbsp finely chopped coriander leaves (cilantro)

Preheat oven to 180°C (350°F).

Lightly oil fish fillet and place in the oven for 15 minutes.

Meanwhile, heat oil in a frying pan over medium-low heat. Add shallot and cook, stirring frequently, until shallot is soft and translucent. Add ginger and cook until fragrant.

Add tomatoes and cook for 10–15 minutes over medium-low heat until sauce becomes thick. Stir frequently so tomatoes don't stick to the pan and dry out. If sauce becomes too thick, add a little water.

Add a pinch of sugar and mix well. Stir in salted soy beans and cook for another 5 minutes over low heat.

Pour sauce over fish fillets and return to the oven for 15–20 minutes until fish is done. Fish should be moist and flake easily when pierced with a fork.

Garnish with coriander and serve with white rice.

Baked Fish

This is another recipe from Sai Aung Tun, my professor friend from Yangon. It is a simple dish, but rich in flavours and aroma. He served it with fried green mango, Shan Sour Rice (page 124), Shan Tomato Salad (page 56), Dried Mustard Soup (page 48), and Watercress with Onion and Garlic (page 110). Just writing about that memorable meal makes me hungry!

SERVES 2

1 firm fleshed white fish, about 700 g (1¹/₂ lb), cleaned and deboned

Salt to taste

2 Tbsp fish sauce

1 Tbsp vegetable oil

1 shallot, peeled and finely chopped

1 clove garlic, peeled and finely chopped

1 Tbsp grated ginger

1 tomato, chopped

2 cups spinach, chopped

2 bird's eye chillies, minced

1 Tbsp mint, chopped

Banana leaf

Rub fish with salt and fish sauce. Leave to marinate for 20 minutes at room temperature or 1 hour in the refrigerator.

Heat oil in a frying pan over medium heat. Add shallot and garlic and cook for about 5 minutes until shallot is translucent.

Preheat oven to 180°C (350°F).

Mix together shallot, garlic, ginger, tomato, spinach, chillies and mint. Stuff into fish.

Lightly scald banana leaf by heating it over an open flame. The leaf will soften and turn a darker shade of green. This will prevent the leaf from tearing.

Wrap fish tightly with banana leaf, then repeat to wrap with aluminium foil. Put into the oven for about 40 minutes until fish is done.

NOTE: Ask the fish monger to debone the fish for you, since it can be a bit tricky to keep the fish intact.

Squeezed Rice with Fish
Htamin Gyin

I got this recipe from a restaurant set in a little hotel in Inle Lake called the Four Sisters Inn. I spent a mesmerising evening watching the proprietresses (who may or may not have been sisters) prepare it. This is a popular dish in the lake region, and it is one of those dishes that everyone makes a little differently. This is my favourite version.

SERVES 4

450 g (1 lb) freshwater fish

Salt to taste

2 large tomatoes, chopped

4-cm (1¹/₂-in) piece tempeh

1 clove garlic, peeled and finely chopped

4 spring onions (scallions), green part only, chopped

2 Tbsp vegetable oil

1 dried chilli

2 cups cooked long-grain rice

1 tsp ground turmeric

3 Tbsp chopped coriander leaves (cilantro)

Bring a large pot of water to the boil. Add fish and boil for about 10 minutes until cooked. Drain and leave to cool. Debone fish and mash.

Bring another pot of water to the boil. Add in 1 tsp salt, then add tomatoes and blanch for about 1 minute. Remove tomatoes and leave to cool before grating into a fine pulp.

Heat a dry pan and roast tempeh for a few minutes. Remove and pound into fine powder using a mortar and pestle. Set aside.

Using the mortar and pestle, pound garlic and spring onions together into a paste.

Heat oil in a pan until smoking. Add garlic and spring onion paste and stir-fry until fragrant, then add mashed fish, mixing gently with a wooden spoon. Add dried chilli and fry until the fish is crisp. Remove from heat.

Place cooked rice in a large bowl. Add fish mixture and grated tomato and mix well.

Shape mixture into balls and sprinkle with tempeh powder.

Serve with a selection of condiments and side dishes such as fish sauce, light soy sauce, tamarind sauce (page 40), finely chopped coriander leaves (cilantro), fried dried chillies, fried tofu, fried pork skin, thin sesame rice wafers and hot and sour vegetable pickles made from pickled turnip, garlic, onions, ginger and mustard greens.

Place a rice ball on your plate and top with a selection of condiments and side dishes. Mix them into the rice ball before eating.

Grilled Fish in Banana Leaf
Par Mok

This absolutely divine recipe came from a woman named Daw Hmwey Sein in Hsipaw. I was exploring the Shan countryside with my friend, Sarah, and translator, Koe Sai Moe, when we heard about a woman who makes an amazing grilled fish parcel. We went to Daw Hmwey Sein's house and watched her at work. She shared with us that she gets up before dawn every morning and makes hundreds of these parcels for sale at the Hsipaw market. She let us try some—rapturous!

SERVES 4

Banana leaves, cut into 4 sheets, each 25-cm (10-in) square

3 tomatoes, finely chopped

8 cups spinach, stems removed and finely chopped

$1/2$ cup coriander leaves (cilantro), finely chopped

3 Tbsp mint, finely chopped

4 spring onions (scallions), ends trimmed and finely chopped

2 cloves garlic, peeled and finely chopped

4 bird's eye chillies, minced

1 Tbsp fish sauce

Salt to taste

2–3 Tbsp vegetable oil

4 white fish fillets, each about 150 g ($5^1/_3$ oz) and 2.5-cm (1-in) thick, cleaned and pat dry

Lightly scald each banana leaf by heating it over an open flame. The leaf will soften and turn a darker shade of green. This will prevent the leaf from tearing.

If grilling, prepare grill. If using oven, preheat to 180°C (350°F).

Using a blender or mortar, mix tomatoes, spinach, coriander, mint, spring onions, garlic, chillies, fish sauce and salt into a paste. Put mixture in a cheese cloth and gently squeeze to remove excess liquid. Remove from cheese cloth and set aside.

Rub banana leaves with a little oil, then place a large spoonful of vegetable paste on leaf. Top with a fish fillet. The fillets can be sliced into smaller pieces, if desired.

Fold banana leaf into a neat parcel. Wrap again with aluminium foil.

If grilling, place parcels over low heat for about 30 minutes, turning regularly to ensure even cooking.

If baking, place parcels in the oven for about 30 minutes until fish is done.

Unwrap and enjoy!

NOTE: If using frozen banana leaves, leave to defrost at room temperature for 5 minutes. Gently peel them apart and cut them with scissors. Omit scalding the leaves as frozen leaves will be more pliable than fresh ones.

Fish Balls with Greens

This recipe comes from the Shan hill town of Kalaw. It originally called for uncooked mustard leaves, but I have substituted with stir-fried Chinese flowering cabbage, which I feel enhance the wonderful flavour of the fish balls. Even if fish balls aren't on your list of favourite foods, be adventurous and try this recipe. I don't think you'll be disappointed!

SERVES 4–6

450 g (1 lb) fish fillet (cod or flounder), minced

1 shallot, peeled and finely chopped

2 cloves garlic, peeled and finely chopped

1 Tbsp grated ginger

3 Tbsp coriander leaves (cilantro), finely chopped

Salt to taste

3 cups vegetable oil

1 bunch Chinese flowering cabbage, cut into short lengths

Put fish, shallot, garlic, ginger, coriander and salt in a bowl and mix with hands. Form into 2.5-cm (1-in) balls.

Heat oil in a deep pan over medium-high heat. When oil is smoking, add fish balls and fry until golden brown. Fish balls should not be cooked through.

Bring water to the boil in a large pot. Add fish balls and boil for about 3 minutes. Remove with a slotted spoon and set aside.

Heat 1 Tbsp oil in a frying pan. Add flowering cabbage and stir-fry until just done and still crisp. Dish out and top with fish balls.

Serve and enjoy!

Stir-fried Eel

This is a traditional dish from Mogok. The spices, especially the anise, make this an unique culinary experience!

SERVES 2

3 Tbsp vegetable oil

2 cloves garlic, peeled and finely chopped

1 eel, about 900 g (2 lb), cut into 5-cm (2-in) pieces

1 head cauliflower, cut into florets

$^1/_4$ tsp anise seed or to taste

$^1/_4$ tsp fish sauce

3 bird's eye chillies, finely chopped

A pinch of ground turmeric

Salt to taste

2 cups bean sprouts, cleaned and chopped

2 Tbsp coriander leaves (cilantro), finely chopped

Heat oil in a frying pan over medium heat. Add garlic and cook until fragrant.

Add eel and stir-fry for 5–10 minutes until done.

Add cauliflower and stir-fry for 5 minutes, then add anise seed, fish sauce, chillies, turmeric and salt to taste.

Stir-fry for 10 minutes or until cauliflower is soft. Add some water to help cook the cauliflower.

Add bean sprouts and stir-fry for another 3–5 minutes. Remove from heat and garnish with coriander. Serve.

NOTE: To prepare eel, cut off the head and remove the skin with a paring knife. Do this by making an incision behind the head. Lift it up with your hands and pull the skin down. Remove as much fat and bones as possible.

Stir-fried Prawns with Tamarind

Tamarind can be a bit sour, and for many it's an acquired taste. But tempered with dried red chillies, shallots and garlic, the sourness takes on a wonderful complexity. I first had this dish at a small restaurant in Inle Lake and knew immediately that I had to get the recipe. Although the Shan typically use small prawns, I find medium prawns carry the flavour better. I love to serve this with white rice and Mango Salad (page 58), as the sweetness of the mango complements the tanginess of the tamarind sauce.

SERVES 4

1 Tbsp vegetable oil

1 shallot, peeled and sliced thinly

1 Tbsp finely chopped garlic

$^1/_2$ cup tamarind liquid (page 40)

1 Tbsp sugar

2 Tbsp fish sauce

6–8 dried red chillies, stems removed and halved

560 g (1$^1/_4$ lb) prawns, peeled and cleaned

2 Tbsp finely chopped coriander leaves (cilantro)

Heat oil in a frying pan. Add shallot and cook until soft and translucent. Add garlic and cook until fragrant.

Add tamarind, sugar, fish sauce and chillies. Stir well.

Bring to the boil, then add prawns and stir-fry for about 5 minutes until prawns turn colour and are cooked.

Garnish with coriander and serve.

meat and Poultry

Although most Shan are Buddhists, meat, primarily pork, chicken and beef is widely eaten. Other meats such as duck, venison and water buffalo are rarely sold at the market, but can be purchased directly from hunters.

Chicken Balls with Pickled Mustard Greens 82

Steamed Ginger Chicken *Jet Tha Pong* 85

Chicken Stir-fried with Leeks *Jet Thaw Jaw* 86

Fried Pork Balls *Wat Tha Lone Jaw* 87

Pork Stew *Nang-Toon* 88

Deep-fried Beef *Zat Byat Byat* 91

Pork in Bamboo *Nayk Larm* 92

Pork with Ginger Tomato Sauce 95

Lemon-Almond Rice 96

Marinated Pork Tenderloin 97

Chicken Balls with Pickled Mustard Greens

I love the combination of pickled mustard greens and chicken balls. Many find pickled mustard greens to be an acquired taste (I admit I was one of them) and never give it a chance. But once you experience it in a delicious dish such as this one, you will be a fan. Give it a try, you may like it!

SERVES 6

2–3 bird's eye chillies, seeded and minced

1 clove garlic, peeled and finely chopped

2.5-cm (1-in) knob ginger, peeled and grated

1 cup plain (all-purpose) flour

Salt and pepper to taste

500 g (1 lb) minced chicken

¼ cup finely chopped coriander leaves (cilantro)

3 cups vegetable oil

¾ cup finely chopped pickled mustard greens

Heat a frying pan over medium heat. Add chillies, garlic and ginger and cook for 3–5 minutes until fragrant. Be careful not to burn garlic. Remove from heat and set aside.

Mix flour with a touch of salt and pepper.

Combine minced chicken with coriander, toasted chillies, garlic and ginger. Mix well. Form chicken mixture into balls about the size of a walnut, then coat with flour. Shake off any excess flour and set aside.

Heat oil in a deep pan over medium-high heat. When oil is smoking, add chicken balls and fry until golden brown and firm. Remove from pan and place on paper towels to drain.

Heat 1 Tbsp oil in a frying pan. Add pickled mustard greens and cook for about 3 minutes until tender but not wilted.

Add chicken balls to pan and cook for 1–2 minutes.

Dish out and garnish with coriander. Serve with white rice.

NOTE: Be careful when cooking chicken. It can appear done on the outside and be raw on the inside. To be sure the chicken balls are cooked all the way through. Break up a chicken ball and check to be very sure.

Steamed Ginger Chicken
Jet Tha Pong

I visited the palace of the deposed Shan royal family in Hsipaw, where I met Donald, the nephew of the former prince. Donald's passion for all things Shan is as strong as his passion for talking! Four hours after I first met him, I managed to get this one recipe. According to Donald, this dish was a royal favourite. "Easy to make and delicious," were his parting words as I fled before he could launch into another soliloquy.

SERVES 4

1 chicken, about 2.25 kg (4^1/$_2$ lb)

^{1}/$_2$ cup fish sauce

1 lemon, halved

12.5-cm (5-in) knob ginger, peeled and cut in half; slice half and grate other half

1 medium yellow onion, peeled and finely chopped

220 g (8 oz) shiitake mushrooms, caps wiped and sliced

Soak a clay pot in water for about 30 minutes. Preheat oven to 190°C (375°F) and place clay pot in oven.

Rinse chicken and pat dry. Rub inside and outside of chicken with fish sauce, then place lemon and sliced ginger into cavity of chicken. Tie chicken legs together with kitchen string.

Combine grated ginger with finely chopped onion and spoon half the mixture into the warmed clay pot.

Lay chicken on top of ginger-onion mixture, then spread remaining ginger-onion mixture over chicken.

Place in the oven and bake for 1^1/$_2$ hours. Remove from oven and serve warm with white rice.

Chicken Stir-fried with Leeks
Jet Thaw Jaw

One cold, rainy day in Mandalay, I was feeling restless and out of sorts, missing home and fighting the urge to hop on the next flight back to the States. Sai Khin insisted that all I really needed was some comfort food, and he bundled me off to one of his favourite restaurants, where he ordered this dish for me. It worked like a dream! I savoured the delicious mild flavours and textures, and by the time I was done, my mood had brightened and I was ready for more adventures.

SERVES 4

2 cups vegetable oil

A pinch of ground turmeric

2 garlic cloves, peeled and finely chopped

2 cups finely chopped boneless chicken breast

2 leeks, ends trimmed, sliced lengthwise, then chopped

5–6 dried chillies, stems and seeds removed

1 tsp sugar

Salt to taste

3 Tbsp finely chopped coriander leaves (cilantro)

Heat oil and turmeric in a frying pan over medium heat. Stir well.

Add garlic and cook for about 3 minutes until just brown. Be careful not to burn garlic.

Add chicken and cook for about 10 minutes until chicken is cooked through.

Add leeks, dried chillies, sugar, and salt. Cook for 10 minutes over medium-low heat, stirring frequently.

Add 1 Tbsp water, reduce heat and cover pan. Cook for another 20 minutes until leeks soften, stirring frequently.

Garnish with coriander and serve with white rice.

Fried Pork Balls
Wat Tha Lone Jaw

I especially enjoy this dish because of the lemon grass. I did not have a lot of lemon grass while in Shan state, therefore, I was pleasantly surprised the first time I tried this. The combination of flavours in this dish make you excuse the fact that it is fried!

SERVES 4

3 cups vegetable oil

2 cloves garlic, peeled and finely chopped

1 Tbsp ginger, peeled and finely chopped

2 Tbsp finely sliced lemon grass

450 g (1 lb) minced pork

1 tomato, finely chopped

1 tsp chilli powder

1 tsp salt

3 Tbsp finely chopped coriander leaves (cilantro)

Heat 1 Tbsp oil in a frying pan over high heat. Add garlic and ginger and cook for 3–4 minutes. Add lemon grass and cook for another 3 minutes. Remove from heat and place in a large bowl.

Place pork, tomato, chilli powder and salt into the bowl and mix well with hands.

Take about one tablespoonful of mixture and form into a ball. Repeat until mixture is used up.

Heat oil in deep pan over high heat. When oil is just starting to smoke, lower in pork balls and fry in batches until golden brown. Takes about 5 minutes. Make sure pork balls are cooked through.

Remove and place on paper towels to absorb excess oil. Garnish with coriander and serve warm.

NOTE: Both fresh and bottled lemon grass can be used.

Pork Stew
Nang-Toon

This dish is traditionally eaten only in the winter months. According to Sai Khin who gave me this recipe, villagers from the countryside make this dish and store it outside in the cold to keep it fresh. It is delicious, easy to make, surprisingly light yet hearty enough to satisfy a hungry stomach!

SERVES 6

$^1/_2$ **cup vegetable oil**

1 yellow onion, peeled and cut into quarters

3 cloves garlic, peeled and finely chopped

2 Tbsp finely chopped ginger

**1 leek, cleaned, halved lengthwise,
    then cut into 1-cm ($^1/_2$-in) pieces**

1 cup plain (all-purpose) flour

Salt and pepper to taste

1.8 kg (4 lb) pork sirloin cutlets, cut into cubes

4 cups chicken stock (page 44)

2 cups water

2 medium white potatoes, peeled and cut into medium-size cubes

1 taro root, peeled and cut into medium size cubes

3 Tbsp finely chopped coriander leaves (cilantro)

Heat 1 Tbsp oil in a frying pan over medium heat. Add onion, garlic, ginger and leek. Stir-fry for about 7 minutes until leek is soft. Be careful not to burn garlic. Set aside.

Mix flour, salt and pepper in a bowl and coat pork.

Heat remaining oil in a frying pan over high heat. Add pork and cook in batches until golden brown on all sides. Drain and place on paper towels to absorb excess oil. Set aside.

Place chicken stock, water, potatoes, taro and stir-fried onion, garlic, ginger and leek mixture in a large pan. Bring to a roaring boil, then reduce heat to simmer and cook uncovered for 2–3 hours. Season to taste with salt and pepper.

Garnish with coriander and serve immediately.

Deep-fried Beef

Zat Byat Byat

This is another recipe from the hill town of Kalaw. At the market early one morning, I struck up a conversation (with the help of my translator) with a group of five Shan women. All five raved about this recipe. After trying it, I understood why. It's scrumptious, if a tad decadent by Western cholesterol-phobic standards.

SERVES 4

4 cups vegetable oil

700 g (1¹/₂ lb) boneless sirloin steak,
   sliced into small, thin strips

1 shallot, peeled and thinly sliced

1 Tbsp grated ginger

3 Tbsp finely chopped coriander leaves (cilantro)

1 lemon or lime, juice extracted (optional)

Salt to taste

Heat oil in a deep pan over medium-high heat. When oil is smoking, add beef and fry in batches until crisp.

Drain beef and place on paper towels to absorb excess oil. Pat dry, then put in a bowl with shallot, ginger, coriander leaves and lemon or lime juice. Mix well and season to taste with salt.

Enjoy with white rice and Mango Salsa (page 37).

NOTE: This recipe originally calls for gooseberry, which adds a touch of sourness to the dish. As gooseberries may be difficult to find, I have used lemon or lime juice which have the same effect.

Pork in Bamboo
Nayk Larm

This dish comes from Mogok (northern Shan state) where it is prepared in a bamboo container covered with straw. I have adapted the recipe for use in the modern kitchen. This dish is a definite must-try!

SERVES 4

1 kg (2 lb 3 oz) pork butt

Plain (all-purpose) flour

Vegetable oil

1 leek, cleaned and halved lengthwise

1 yellow onion, peeled and finely chopped

1 clove garlic, peeled and finely chopped

1 large tomato, halved, seeds removed
   and finely chopped

1/2 cup finely chopped coriander leaves (cilantro)

2 tsp ground turmeric

2 tsp sugar

1 tsp salt

1 tsp chilli powder

1 tsp fermented black beans, toasted and ground

1 cup chicken stock (page 44)

Trim fat from pork and remove any connective tissue. Cut pork into strips, then into medium-size cubes.

In a large bowl, add enough flour for coating pork. Add pork and coat well.

Heat 4 Tbsp oil in a large frying pan over medium-high heat. Add pork and sear in batches until golden brown on all sides. Dish out and set aside.

Reheat the same pan over medium heat. Add leek, onion and garlic and stir-fry for 5–8 minutes until onion is soft. Add some oil if necessary.

Add tomato, coriander leaves, turmeric, sugar, salt, chilli powder and fermented black beans. Stir well. Remove pan from heat and set aside.

Preheat oven to 180°C (350°F).

Cut pork into smaller bite-size pieces and return to pan with vegetables. Add chicken stock and place over medium heat until simmering.

Cover pan and put in the oven to bake for 1 1/2 hours.

Adjust seasoning to taste and serve hot with rice or noodles.

Pork with Ginger Tomato Sauce

One morning at the market in Kalaw, I came across a brown spice powder I had never seen before. The vendor told me it was *mat khaut*, made from the bark of a rare tree that grows only in Shan state. Intrigued, I asked him how it is used and he gave me this recipe. He also explained that because *mat khaut* is becoming difficult to find even in Shan state, it is often omitted, but this dish tastes as delicious without it. Although I do not know what it tastes like with *mat khaut*, I agree that this dish is delectable indeed!

SERVES 4

1.8 kg (4 lb) pork butt

1 cup plain (all-purpose) or chickpea flour

1 cup vegetable oil

1 kg (2 lb 3 oz) large ripe tomatoes

1 medium yellow onion, peeled and chopped

4 cloves garlic, peeled and finely chopped

5-cm (2-in) knob ginger, peeled and grated

Salt and pepper to taste

2 cups chicken stock (page 44)

¹/₂ cup coriander leaves (cilantro), finely chopped

Trim fat from pork. Cut pork into 4-cm (1¹/₂-in) cubes. Place flour in a large bowl and coat pork. Shake off remaining flour.

Heat ¹/₄ cup oil in a large frying pan over medium heat. When smoking, add pork and cook in batches until golden brown on all sides, but not cooked through. Remove pork and set aside.

Bring a pot of water to the boil and blanch tomatoes for about 1 minute. Drain and place in a bowl of cold water. Gently peel tomatoes, then cut into quarters. Remove seeds and pulp and finely chop.

Heat 2 Tbsp oil in a large casserole dish over medium-high heat. Add onion, garlic and ginger and cook for about 5 minutes until onion is soft. Lower heat if necessary.

Add tomatoes, 1 tsp salt and ¹/₂ tsp black pepper. Cook for about 10 minutes for tomatoes to release juices and for juices to slightly evaporate.

Add pork, chicken stock and coriander leaves and bring to the boil. Reduce heat to a simmer and cook covered for 45 minutes to 1 hour. Stir occasionally to keep pork from sticking to the bottom of the casserole.

Adjust seasoning to taste and serve. This dish goes well with Lemon-Almond Rice (page 96).

Lemon-Almond Rice

SERVES 4

**3 cups chicken stock (page 44)
   or water**

1^1/$_2$ cups long-grain rice

**1 lemon, grated for zest and
   juice extracted**

^{1}/$_2$ cup sliced almonds, lightly toasted

**3 spring onions (scallions),
   finely chopped**

1 tsp salt

^{1}/$_2$ tsp ground black pepper

Bring chicken stock or water to the boil over high heat. Add rice, cover and cook for about 20 minutes or until rice is light and fluffy.

Add lemon zest and juice, almonds, spring onions, salt and pepper. Lightly stir with a fork to mix.

Adjust seasoning if necessary and serve.

Marinated Pork Tenderloin

Until I came across this recipe, I had never had pork marinated with mint and ginger. What a revelation! It is especially tasty when combined with garlic, lime and coriander. This can be cooked on the grill or in the oven, but the Shan almost always grill it. Serve with Long Bean Stir-fry (page 111), Mushroom Salad (page 61) and Mango Salsa (page 37) and you will be in food heaven!

SERVES 6

1–1.5 kg (2 lb 3 oz–3 lb 4¹/₂ oz) pork tenderloin

2 cloves garlic, peeled and finely chopped

1 shallot, peeled and finely chopped

2.5-cm (1-in) knob ginger, peeled and grated

³/₄ cup coriander leaves (cilantro), finely chopped

³/₄ cup mint, finely chopped

2 Tbsp fish sauce

3 Tbsp vegetable oil

2 Tbsp lime juice

2 Tbsp white rice vinegar

Salt to taste

Start preparations at least 3 hours ahead.

Combine all ingredients in a plastic bag and seal. Massage ingredients into pork and refrigerate for at least 3 hours and up to 24 hours.

Remove pork from bag and discard marinade.

Preheat oven to 180°C (350°F) or heat grill.

If roasting, heat a pan and sear pork on all sides to brown, then place in the oven for 15–20 minutes. Remove and let rest for 5 minutes before serving.

If grilling, sear pork on all sides on the hot grill, then lower heat and cook until meat is done. Remove and let rest for 5 minutes before serving.

Slice and enjoy!

Tofu and Vegetables

Vegetable and tofu dishes are a staple of the Shan diet. A variety of tofu is also available in the Shan state. This includes a yellow tofu, made of split pea flour, that is indigenous to Myanmar and is rarely seen outside the country. I have suggested substitutes in the following recipes where the ingredients may not be readily available outside of Myanmar.

Fried Tofu Salad
To Hpu Gyaw Thouk

I was at the market in Hsipaw early one morning and all the colourful, sensual foods on display made me ravenous. I sat down at a tiny food stall, on a stool more fitting for a mouse, and watched as an older Shan woman prepared this mouthwatering dish of Shan tofu. Made from split pea flour, Shan tofu is pleasantly light with a slight nutty aftertaste. In this salad, the mélange of spices blended with the fried tofu—crisp on the outside with a melt-in-your-mouth middle—makes this dish another must-try!

SERVES 4

280 g (10 oz) yellow tofu (page 105)
    or compressed tofu

¹/₄ cup vegetable oil

1 clove garlic, peeled and finely chopped

1 shallot, peeled and thinly sliced

2 cups canned whole tomatoes or
    4 fresh tomatoes, chopped

2–3 Tbsp lemon or lime juice

Salt to taste

³/₄ cup coriander leaves (cilantro),
    finely chopped

Drain tofu and pat dry with paper towels. Slice tofu into 18 pieces, each about 0.5-cm (¹/₄-in) thick.

Heat oil in a deep pan over medium-high heat. Carefully lower tofu into hot oil and fry for 3–4 minutes until browned on all sides. Remove from pan and place on paper towels to absorb excess oil. Set aside on a serving plate.

Leaving just 1 Tbsp oil in the pan, reheat over medium heat. Add garlic and shallot and cook until shallot is tender. Be careful not to burn garlic. Add tomatoes and simmer until mixture thickens. Takes 10–20 minutes. Stir in lemon or lime juice. Season with salt to taste.

Pour sauce over tofu and gently mix. Garnish with coriander leaves and serve.

NOTE: The Shan use a yellow tofu (won ta hpo) made from yellow split peas. Compressed tofu makes an acceptable substitute.

Shan Tofu Salad
To Hpu Thouk

This light, refreshing salad made with Shan tofu and savoury spices, goes well with steamed fish and warm rice. It is on the menu in every restaurant in Shan state, and more or less their equivalent to the ubiquitous Western green salad.

SERVES 4

1 cup vegetable oil

1 clove garlic, peeled and finely chopped

1 Tbsp red chilli flakes

**280 g (10 oz) yellow tofu (page 105)
   or compressed tofu**

2 spring onions (scallions), finely chopped

**3 Tbsp coriander leaves (cilantro),
   finely chopped**

3 Tbsp unsalted toasted peanuts

1 tsp sugar

1 Tbsp light soy sauce

1 Tbsp white rice vinegar

Salt to taste

Start preparations a few hours ahead.

Heat 1 Tbsp oil in a frying pan over medium heat. Add garlic and cook for until browned. Remove from heat and set aside.

Heat remaining oil in a pan. When warm, pour oil equally into 2 glass jars. Add cooked garlic to one and chilli flakes to the other jar. Put lids on jars and let steep for several hours.

Slice tofu into thin pieces. Put into a bowl and add 1–2 tsp garlic and chilli flake oils. Add remaining ingredients and toss gently to combine. Season with salt to taste and serve immediately.

NOTE: The chilli flake oil will keep indefinitely, sealed in the clean glass gar. The garlic oil, however, should be discarded, as harmful bacteria can build up on the garlic if it is stored for long in oil.

Bean Sprouts with Tofu

Pae Pin Pout / Pae Pya Jaw

I first tasted this at a wonderful restaurant in Mandalay called Lashio Lay, where I quickly became a regular. The play of soft tofu and crunchy bean sprouts is delightful. It's amazing that a dish this simple can be so satisfying.

SERVES 4

2 Tbsp vegetable oil

1 clove garlic, peeled and finely chopped

2–3 bird's eye chillies, minced

1 small green capsicum (bell pepper),
   cored and chopped

280 g (10 oz) yellow tofu (page 105) or
   compressed tofu, cut into 2.5-cm (1-in) cubes

2 medium tomatoes, chopped

1 tsp sugar (optional)

Salt to taste

4 cups bean sprouts

Heat oil in a frying pan over medium heat. Add garlic, chillies and capsicum and cook until capsicum is soft. Be careful not to burn garlic and chillies.

Add tofu and cook until golden brown on all sides.

Add tomatoes and cook for about 3 minutes until soft. Add a pinch of sugar and salt to taste.

Add bean sprouts and stir-fry until bean sprouts are warm but not wilted.

Dish out and serve immediately.

NOTE: Bean sprouts should have a bright white colour and be dry and crisp. If they are turning brown, are limp or damp, discard and do not use.

Twice-fried Tofu Fritters

Hnapyan Gyaw

This marvellous dish is enough to make anyone a fan of deep-frying. After the first deep-fry, the tofu is drained, slit halfway down the middle and fried again. It is generally served as a side dish, but I love it as a main course mixed with white rice and topped with Shan Tomato Salad (page 57)!

SERVES 4

3 cups vegetable oil

Yellow Tofu

2 cups dried yellow split peas

1 tsp ground turmeric

5–6 cups water

Salt to taste

Start preparations for the yellow tofu a day ahead. Place split peas in stainless steel bowl and cover with water. Leave to soak overnight.

The following day, drain peas and put into a blender. Process into a smooth paste. Transfer paste to a large pot. Add 3 cups water and place over medium-low heat, whisking constantly to keep mixture from sticking to the bottom of the pot. As mixture heats, it will thicken to the consistency of thick porridge. This should take 15–20 minutes. If the mixture becomes too thick, add more water. Leave to cool, then refrigerate until set. Take about 1 hour. Cut tofu into rectangular pieces about 1.5-cm (¼-in) thick.

Heat oil in a deep pan over medium-high heat. When oil is smoking, add tofu in batches and fry until golden brown on all sides.

Drain tofu and place onto paper towels to absorb excess oil.

Make a cut in the middle of each tofu rectangle and fry again. Drain on paper towels.

Enjoy with Mango Salsa (page 37), Vinegar and Sesame Dip (page 38) or Tamarind Sauce (page 40).

Warm Tofu with Rice Noodles
To Hpu Nway

This is a very popular snack. The creamy tofu is kept warm in a big vat or pot, then poured over rice noodles and topped with various garnishes such as peanuts and chillies. It can also be mixed with fried tofu and garnished with mange tout vine (pea tendrils). I loved watching the Shan people eat this dish because there is a real "art" to eating it gracefully—an art I haven't quite mastered, but this dish is delicious nonetheless!

SERVES 4–6

Creamy Yellow Tofu

2 cups dried yellow split peas

1 tsp ground turmeric

5–6 cups water

Salt to taste

Rice Noodles

8 cups water

1 tsp salt

1 Tbsp vegetable oil

225 g (8 oz) medium width flat rice noodles

Condiments

2 cups unsalted toasted peanuts, chopped

1 Tbsp crushed garlic

¼ cup coriander leaves (cilantro), chopped

¼ cup pickled mustard greens or mange tout vine

1 tsp chilli oil

1 tsp dark soy sauce

1 tsp rice vinegar

1 cup pork rind

Start preparations for the yellow tofu a day ahead. Place split peas in stainless steel bowl and cover with water. Leave to soak overnight.

The following day, drain peas and put into a blender. Process into a smooth paste. Transfer paste to a large pot. Add 3 cups water and place over medium-low heat, whisking constantly to keep mixture from sticking to the bottom of the pot. As mixture heats, it will thicken to the consistency of thick porridge. This should take 15–20 minutes. If the mixture becomes too thick, add more water. Cover and keep warm.

Prepare noodles. Bring the water to the boil. Add salt and oil and remove from heat. Add noodles to hot water and leave for 3–5 minutes until noodles are tender. Drain noodles and place in a bowl. Keep covered until ready to serve.

To serve, place a small handful of noodles in a serving bowl. Top with some tofu and mix well. Serve with your choice of condiments.

Tofu Parcel
Tofu Mok

Sai Aung Tun, a history professor at Yangon University, is not only a brilliant historian, but quite the foodie too! As a little boy growing up in the Shan state, he collected recipes from his mother and grandmothers. Sai Aung was kind enough to take me under his wing; he sent me as far as Chiang Mai in Thailand to learn about Shan food, and his referrals always earned me a warm welcome. I was a frequent dinner guest at his house and, as you can imagine, spent much time in the kitchen. This dish, which is a bit like a frittata, is one of his favourites and I hope it will soon to be one of yours.

SERVES 4–6

280 g (10 oz) tofu

1 egg

2 cloves garlic, peeled and finely chopped

2 green bird's eye chilies, minced

3 whole tomatoes, finely chopped

1 shallot, peeled and finely chopped

1 Tbsp fish sauce

Salt to taste

Banana leaves, cut into 13 x 13-cm (5 x 5-in) sheets

Preheat oven to 180°C (350°F).

Mash tofu in a large bowl. Add egg and mix well. Add garlic, chillies, tomatoes, shallot and fish sauce. Mix well. Season with salt.

Drop a spoonful of the mixture onto a banana leaf. Fold two opposite sides of banana leaf over filling, then fold the open ends downwards to enclose filling. Place on a baking tray. Repeat with remaining filling.

Bake for about 20 minutes.

Unwrap and enjoy!

Watercress with Onion and Garlic

Ka Zum Yent Kyaw

Not only is watercress high in calcium and vitamin C, it is also a very tasty vegetable with a distinctive touch of bitterness that adds interest to the dish it is used in. The combination of watercress, onion, ginger, chillies and garlic in this recipe makes this a perfect side for any meat or fish dish.

SERVES 4

1 Tbsp vegetable oil

1 Tbsp garlic, peeled and finely chopped

1 medium yellow onion, peeled and finely chopped

1 tsp minced bird's eye chilli (optional)

1 tsp grated ginger

3 cups watercress, cleaned, stems and leaves separated

1 tsp fish sauce

Salt to taste

Heat oil in a frying pan over medium heat. Add garlic, onion, chilli and ginger. Cook until onion is translucent. Be careful not to burn garlic.

Add watercress stems and stir-fry until wilted. Takes about 2 minutes.

Add watercress leaves and stir-fry until wilted. Takes about 1 minute.

Season with fish sauce and salt to taste.

Dish out and serve at room temperature.

NOTE: Watercress is highly perishable and should be used on the day of purchase.

Long Bean Stir-fry
Pae Thee Kyaw

It's hard to go wrong with stir-fried long beans, especially when they are smothered in a light tomato sauce with a touch of garlic. Chinese long beans are abundant throughout Myanmar, but their flavour is a little mild and they lack the crispy snap of Western green beans. Long beans and green beans work equally well in this recipe.

SERVES 6

450 g (1 lb) long beans or green beans, ends trimmed

1 Tbsp vegetable oil

1 yellow onion, peeled and finely chopped

1 clove garlic, peeled and finely chopped

2 medium tomatoes, chopped

Salt to taste

Bring a large pot of water to the boil. Add beans and cook until tender. Takes 5–10 minutes. Drain beans and set aside.

Heat oil in a frying pan over medium heat. Add onion and garlic and stir-fry until onion is translucent. Be careful not to burn garlic.

Add tomatoes and cook for about 10 minutes until tomatoes are mushy. Add beans and mix.

Add 1 tsp warm water to the pan and cover for about 1 minute. Season with salt to taste.

Dish out and serve.

Stir-fried Aubergines with Salted Fish

Kha Yean Thee Nga Kyaw

This is a uniquely Shan recipe. The sweetness of the onion and aubergine contrasts with the saltiness of the fish to delicious effect. This works well as a side dish and can also be served on its own with a big bowl of steaming hot rice.

SERVES 4

450 g (1 lb) salted fish

2 Tbsp vegetable or sesame oil

1 yellow onion, peeled and finely chopped

1 clove garlic, peeled and finely chopped

2 medium tomatoes, chopped

**1 large aubergine (eggplant/brinjal), peeled
    and cut into 2.5-cm (1-in) cubes**

1 Tbsp coriander leaves (cilantro), finely chopped

Salt to taste

Start preparations a day ahead. Soak fish in water and leave overnight. Change the water every 2–4 hours if possible.

The following day, drain fish and pat dry. Cut into 2.5-cm (1-in) squares.

Heat oil in a frying pan. Add salted fish, onion, garlic and tomatoes. Cook for 10–15 minutes until sauce thickens slightly.

Add aubergine and cook until soft.

Dish out and garnish with coriander. Serve immediately.

Fried Mango Rice
Tha Yet Thee Kyaw

My historian friend, Sai Aung Tun, serves me this dish whenever he invites me over for dinner. He adores it, and so do I. The combination of sweet mango and hot chillies is lively and intriguing, I always serve this when I have vegetarian friends over.

SERVES 4

2 Tbsp vegetable oil

2 cloves garlic, peeled and sliced

1 purple onion, peeled and thinly sliced

3 bird's eye chillies, finely chopped

**1 medium mango (not completely ripe; a bit hard),
   peeled and sliced**

**1 medium green capsicum (bell pepper)
   cored and sliced**

Salt to taste

1 tsp sugar (optional)

2 cups cooked long-grain rice

2 Tbsp chopped coriander leaves (cilantro)

Heat oil in a pan over medium heat. Add garlic, onion and chillies and stir-fry for about 5 minutes. Be careful not to burn garlic.

Add mango, capsicum, salt and sugar. Stir-fry for 10–15 minutes to cook capsicum lightly.

Add rice and mix well. Cook for another 5–10 minutes.

Dish out and let sit for about 5 minutes. Garnish with coriander and serve.

Vegetable Fritters

Fresh vegetables are served together with every Shan meal. They are typically served on the side for nibbling on throughout the meal, but are sometimes also made into these delicious fritters, which I first tasted at a friend's house in Yangon. He would shop for the freshest vegetables and turn them into fritters for serving with dips. Delicious!

SERVES 4

4 eggs

A mix of vegetables such as aubergine (eggplant/brinjal), pumpkin, carrot, sweet potato, taro and long beans, peeled if necessary and sliced or cut into sticks

¹/₂ cup plain (all–purpose) flour

3 cups vegetable oil

Salt to taste

Whisk eggs together until completely blended and smooth.

Dip vegetables into egg, then coat lightly with flour.

Heat oil in a deep pan over high heat. When oil is smoking, add vegetables in small batches and fry until golden brown.

Use a slotted spoon to remove vegetables. Place on paper towels to absorb excess oil. Pat dry.

Arrange fritters on a serving plate and sprinkle with salt. Serve with Spicy Pork Dip (page 41).

Street Food

I enjoyed eating Shan street food because it was fast, fresh and lively. There was an element of theatre to sit at a tiny sidewalk counter and watch your food prepared in front of your eyes, in a wok or over a wood-burning stove, and then to eat it as you watch the vibrant street life around you. A variety of food was available, from noodles and baked fish, to sweets and hot tea, and many of the cooks embellished the dishes with their personal flair.

Shan Noodles
Khaut Swe

I got this recipe from the proprietress of a market food stall in Kyauq Mei, a town in Shan state. I enjoyed watching her prepare the dish and talk me through the process. Shan noodles are popularly eaten for breakfast, lunch and dinner. If extra sustenance is needed, sticky noodles are preferred over rice noodles because, according to the Shan, they 'stick to your bones' better.

SERVES 4

400 g (14$^{1}/_{3}$ oz) flat rice vermicelli

3 Tbsp vegetable oil

1 shallot, peeled and thinly sliced

3 garlic cloves, peeled and finely chopped

1 tsp grated ginger

1 tsp chilli powder

2 boneless chicken breasts, minced

220 g (8 oz) can whole tomatoes or
    3 medium tomatoes, chopped

Salt to taste

1 cup thick sweet soy sauce

$^{1}/_{4}$ cup unsalted roasted peanuts, finely chopped

3 Tbsp finely chopped spring onion (scallion)

Bring water to the boil in a pot. Remove pot from heat and place rice vermicelli in to cook and soften. Vermicelli should be soft but not mushy. Drain and rinse with cool water. Set aside.

Heat 1 Tbsp oil in a pan over medium heat. Add shallot, garlic, ginger and chilli powder. Cook until shallots are soft. Add chicken and mix well. When chicken is done, add tomatoes and cook over low heat, stirring frequently until tomato juices thicken. Season to taste with salt.

Divide vermicelli among 4 serving bowls. Add enough sweet soy sauce to cover vermicelli, then top with peanuts and spring onion.

NOTE: There are several different sizes of rice noodles, from very thin (vermicelli) to very wide (*hor fun*). Choose a noodle based on your taste and preferences, but note that heavier sauces, like those made with tomatoes and chunks of meat, tend to pair better with wider noodles and vinaigrettes and lighter sauces work marvellously with thinner noodles.

Shan Rice Noodles
Kow Sen

This is a popular noodle dish in Shan state and like many other noodle dishes, it has many variations. No matter how many times I tried this dish there, it was never the same! This is my favourite version of the dish.

SERVES 4

2 Tbsp vegetable oil

1 medium yellow onion, peeled and chopped

3 garlic cloves, peeled and finely chopped

2.5-cm (1-in) knob ginger, peeled and grated

2 tsp ground turmeric

450 g (1 lb) minced pork

2 tomatoes, chopped

1/2 cup coriander leaves (cilantro), finely chopped

2 tsp light soy sauce

1 cup chicken stock (page 44)

6 cups water

400 g (14 1/3 oz) dried coarse rice vermicelli

Garnish

1/2 cup chopped spring onions (scallions)

1 lime, cut into quarters

1 cup pork rind

4 Tbsp white sesame seeds, toasted

Heat oil in a frying pan over medium heat. Add onion and cook until translucent, then add garlic and ginger. Lower heat and cook for another 5 minutes.

Add turmeric and minced pork. Stir-fry to mix. When pork is cooked, add tomatoes, coriander, soy sauce and chicken stock. Simmer for 20 minutes until liquid is reduced by half. Remove from heat and keep warm.

Bring water to the boil in a pot. Remove pot from heat and add rice vermicelli to cook and soften. Vermicelli should be soft but not mushy. Drain and rinse with cool water.

Divide vermicelli among 4 serving bowls. Ladle sauce into bowls over vermicelli and garnish with spring onions, lime, pork rind and sesame seeds. Serve immediately.

Shan Noodle Soup
Shan Hkauk Swe

The Shan love noodles and I must have tried at least two dozen variations!
This is one of my favourites. It is the Shan version of chicken noodle soup,
warming and deeply satisfying.

SERVES 4

280 (10 oz) yellow tofu (page 105) or compressed tofu, drained

5 Tbsp vegetable oil

1 boneless chicken breast, cut into small cubes

Salt and pepper to taste

500 g (1 lb 1½ oz) flat rice noodles

4 cups chicken stock (page 44)

2 tsp chilli oil

2 tsp light soy sauce

Garnish

2 Tbsp unsalted roasted peanuts, crushed

1 Tbsp white sesame seeds, toasted

3 Tbsp mange tout vine or coriander leaves (cilantro),
　　finely chopped with stems removed

Pat tofu dry with paper towels, then cut into 18 pieces, each about 0.5-cm
(¼-in) thick.

Heat 4 Tbsp oil in a deep pan over medium-high heat. When oil is smoking, add
tofu and fry for 3–4 minutes until browned on all sides. Remove from pan and
place on paper towels to absorb excess oil. Set aside.

Discard excess oil from pan and wipe pan with paper towels. Place pan over
medium heat and add remaining oil. When oil is hot, add chicken and stir-fry until
done. Season with salt and pepper to taste. Remove from heat and set aside.

Bring a pot of water to the boil. Remove pot from heat and place noodles in to
cook and soften. Noodles should be soft but not mushy. Drain and rinse with cool
water. Set aside.

Warm chicken stock, but do not bring to the boil. Add salt to taste.

Divide noodles among 4 serving bowls. Ladle chicken stock over, then top with
chicken, fried tofu, chilli oil, light soy sauce and salt to taste. Mix.

Garnish with peanuts, sesame seeds and mange tout vine or coriander leaves.
Serve immediately.

Shan Sour Rice
Hta Min Chin

This dish is a family favourite of my Shan friend, Minge. I spent a delightful evening in her kitchen learning how to make it. There are many variations of Shan sour rice, but this is the one I like best. These tangy rice balls smothered with a savoury chicken sauce never fail to wow my dinner guests!

SERVES 6

Rice Balls

2 medium white potatoes

900 g (2 lb) canned whole tomatoes or 5 fresh tomatoes

4 Tbsp vegetable oil

1 tsp ground turmeric

3 cups freshly cooked long-grain rice

3 cloves garlic, peeled and finely chopped

1 shallot, peeled and finely chopped

1 tsp ground turmeric

1 tsp red chilli powder

2 Tbsp dried black bean powder (page 39) (optional)

Salt to taste

2 boneless chicken breasts, finely chopped

$1/4$ cup unsalted roasted peanuts, coarsely chopped

3 Tbsp finely chopped coriander leaves (cilantro)

Prepare rice balls. Bring a large pot of water to the boil and boil potatoes until tender. Takes 30–45 minutes. Drain and leave to cool. Peel potatoes and mash. Set aside.

If using fresh tomatoes, blanch them in a pot of boiling water for about 1 minute. Drain, then place in a bowl of cool water. Peel skins and set aside.

Heat 2 Tbsp oil over medium heat. Add a pinch of turmeric and stir for about 1 minute. Remove from heat and pour into a large bowl. Add cooked rice, 2 tomatoes and potatoes to bowl and mix well with hands. Mixture should be sticky.

Form mixture into balls about the size of a peach. Place on a serving plate and cover with aluminium foil to keep warm. (The rice balls can be placed in an oven preheated to 100°C (210°F) to warm up if desired.)

Prepare sauce. Heat oil in a frying pan over medium heat. Add garlic, shallot, remaining turmeric, chilli powder, dried black bean powder, if using, and salt. Cook, stirring frequently, until shallot is soft. Be careful not to burn garlic.

Add remaining tomatoes and chicken and cook over low heat, stirring frequently, until mixture starts to thicken.

Pour tomato sauce over rice balls. Garnish with peanuts and coriander.

Shan Rolls

Shan Laik

Shan rolls are one of my favourite snacks. I discovered them at a food cart stationed near where I was staying in Yangon. It was run by a Shan family who would set up their bright blue cart every morning. They served some of the best food I have ever tried in Myanmar. Their crisp, golden Shan rolls were filled with tofu, sprouts and spring onions, and a tamarind sauce or vinegar and sesame dip completed the treat!|

MAKES 12 ROLLS

**280 g (10 oz) extra firm or
compressed tofu, drained**

**2 cups bean sprouts or garlic stems,
finely chopped**

**3 cups spring onions (scallions),
finely chopped**

Salt to taste

12 wonton wrappers

3 cups vegetable oil

**A few sprigs of coriander
leaves (cilantro)**

Pat tofu dry, then cut into small cubes. Place in a bowl with bean sprouts or garlic stems, spring onions and salt to taste. Mix well.

Lay a wonton wrapper on a flat work surface. Spoon a small amount of mixture in the middle, then fold the left and right sides of the wonton wrapper over the filling. Fold the bottom edge of the wrapper over the filling, then roll the parcel up neatly. Seal the parcel using a little water. Repeat until the ingredients are used up.

Heat oil in deep pan over medium-high heat. When oil is smoking, add rolls in batches and fry until golden brown.

Remove with a slotted spoon and place on paper towels to absorb excess oil.

Garnish with coriander leaves and serve with Tamarind Sauce (page 40) or Vinegar and Sesame Dip (page 38) on the side.

Spring Onion Fritters
Chin Baung Kyaw

This is a traditional Shan snack from the Inle Lake region. I first tasted this yummy snack when it was being prepared for a lavish wedding feast. I hung out in the kitchen and was appointed unofficial taster. What a delightful afternoon that was! Although I call it a snack, the Shan also have it for breakfast, lunch and dinner with noodles.

SERVES 4

2 cloves garlic, peeled and finely chopped

2.5-cm (1-in) knob ginger, peeled and finely chopped

3–4 spring onions (scallions), finely chopped

2 Tbsp rice flour

Salt to taste

1 Tbsp chilli powder or sauce

1 tsp sugar or liquid jaggery (palm sugar)

3 cups vegetable oil

A few sprigs of coriander leaves (cilantro)

Combine garlic, ginger and spring onions with rice flour, salt, chilli powder or sauce and sugar in a bowl. Mix well into a paste. Add some water if mixture is too dry.

Heat oil in a deep pan over high heat. When oil is smoking, drop spoonfuls of mixture into oil and fry in batches until golden brown. Repeat until mixture is used up.

Remove balls with a slotted spoon and place on paper towels to absorb excess oil.

Garnish with coriander. Serve with white rice and hot green tea.

Pork in Banana Leaf
Ka Yan Huei

This snack comes from Eastern Shan State, and was my favourite treat to nibble on while perusing markets on chilly mornings. According to the woman at whose stand I first tasted this, *ka yan huei* is popular among farmers and field workers because it is both filling and tasty. Most Shan eat this using their fingers.

SERVES 4–6

1 Tbsp vegetable oil

1 clove garlic, peeled and finely chopped

1 shallot, peeled and finely chopped

450 g (1 lb) minced pork

1 tsp ground turmeric

Salt to taste

Banana leaves, cut into 6 square sheets, each about 25 cm (10 in)

4 cups cooked sticky (glutinous) rice

3 Tbsp chopped coriander leaves (cilantro)

Preheat oven to 180°C (350°F).

Heat oil in a frying pan over medium-low heat. Add garlic and shallot and stir-fry until fragrant. Remove to a medium bowl.

Add pork and turmeric to bowl and mix well. Season to taste with salt. Divide into 6 portions.

Divide sticky rice into 6 portions and spoon a portion onto the middle of a banana leaf. Flatten mould of rice slightly, then top with a portion of pork mixture. Garnish with coriander. Fold two opposite sides of banana leaf over filling to enclose it, then fold open ends down, so the weight of the parcel sits on them, securing the parcel. Repeat to make 6 parcels.

Put parcels on a baking tray and place in the oven for 25–30 minutes until pork is thoroughly cooked.

Unwrap and eat!

Potato and Rice Steamed in Banana Leaves

I came across this recipe while visiting Hsipaw. I was a bit lost, wandering the streets trying to find my hotel, when suddenly the most wonderful smell wafted towards me. Following my nose, I came upon a man making this dish at his tiny food stall. One taste and I was hooked. Since I was without a translator, I used hand signals to ask him if he would make the dish in front of me, and he cheerfully agreed. It's Shan comfort food, and it makes a perfect accompaniment to a meat or fish meal.

SERVES 4–6

3 medium white potatoes

2 Tbsp vegetable oil

2 shallots, peeled and thinly sliced

3 cloves garlic, peeled and thinly sliced

8–9 dried chillies, stems removed

3 medium tomatoes, chopped

**2 cups spinach leaves, cleaned and
    finely chopped**

Salt to taste

**Banana leaves, cut into 4 square sheets,
    each about 25 cm (10 in)**

4 cups cooked sticky (glutinous) rice

Bring a large pot of water to the boil and cook potatoes until soft. Takes about 30 minutes. Drain and cool, then peel and cut into small cubes. Set aside.

Heat oil in a frying pan over medium heat. Add shallots and cook for about 4 minutes until soft. Reduce heat to medium-low and add garlic and chillies and cook for another 5 minutes, being careful not to burn garlic.

Add tomatoes and spinach and cook for about 10 minutes. Add potatoes and cook for another 5 minutes, stirring frequently. Season to taste with salt. Remove from heat and divide into 4 portions.

Preheat oven to 180°C (350°F).

Divide sticky rice into 4 portions and spoon a portion onto the middle of a banana leaf. Flatten mould of rice slightly, then top with a portion of potato mixture. Fold two opposite sides of banana leaf over filling to enclose it, then fold open ends down, so the weight of the parcel sits on them, securing the parcel. Repeat to make 4 parcels.

Put parcels on a baking tray and place in the oven for about 20 minutes.

Unwrap and eat!

Banana with Coconut Rice

Nya Bin Kau Ni

The Shan have a sweet tooth and they have many scrumptious sweet recipes. This particular snack/dessert is very popular at traditional Shan ceremonies, as well as in the marketplace. It is one of my favourites as I love bananas.

SERVES 4

2 cups cooked sticky (glutinous) rice

1 cup grated coconut

3 Tbsp sugar or to taste

Banana leaves, cut into 4 square sheets, each about 25 cm (10 in)

3 bananas, peeled, cut across in half, then halved again lengthwise

Preheat oven to 180°C (350°F).

Mix together rice, coconut and sugar in a bowl. Divide into 4 portions.

Spoon a portion of rice mixture onto the middle of a banana leaf. Flatten mould of rice slightly, then top with 3 pieces of banana. Fold two opposite sides of banana leaf over filling to enclose it, then fold open ends down, so the weight of the parcel sits on them, securing the parcel. Repeat to make 4 parcels.

Put parcels on a baking tray and place in the oven for 20–25 minutes until banana is soft.

Unwrap and eat!

Sticky Rice Snack
Khou Pooke

This snack is traditionally served at various Shan ceremonies, such as that to celebrate the winter season or the Shan New Year. As it is such a popular snack, some villagers also have it for breakfast. It can be deep-fried and served with pickled mustard, peas and tofu. My preference is to enjoy it plain with a hot cup of tea.

MAKES A 20 X 12-CM (5 X 8-IN) BLOCK

¹/₄ cup white sesame seeds, toasted

Salt to taste

1 cup cooked sticky (glutinous) rice

¹/₄ cup honey, warmed

Line a 20 x 12-cm (5 x 8-in) tray with plastic wrap.

Using a mortar and pestle or a blender, grind or process sesame seeds with a pinch of salt until fine. Add rice and honey and continue to grind or process into a sticky mass.

Transfer mixture to lined tray and spread it out into a 2.5-cm (1-in) thick layer. Cover with plastic wrap and refrigerate until firm. Takes about 1 hour. Once firm, slice and enjoy. The strips can also be deep-fried, if desired.

Golden Rice
Suay Tamin

This snack/dessert is a bit like tapioca pudding. The Shan cook it over an open fire, but I have adapted it for cooking in the oven which may be more suitable for the modern kitchen.

YIELDS 3 CUPS

390 g (14 oz) can unsweetened coconut milk

1/4 cup sugar

1 tsp vanilla essence

A pinch of salt

1 cup cooked sticky (glutinous) rice

1/4 cup toasted sweetened coconut flakes

Preheat oven to 180°C (350°F).

Heat coconut milk in a heatproof pan over low heat. Bring to a simmer, then add sugar, vanilla and salt, stirring to dissolve sugar.

Add rice to pan and mix. Cover with a lid and put in the oven for 20 minutes.

Remove pan from oven and stir in toasted coconut flakes. Serve warm or cold. To serve cold, transfer rice to a lined loaf tin and flatten it. Refrigerate for about 2 hours until firm, then cut into strips and enjoy!

Glossary

Bamboo Shoots

Bean Sprouts

Bird's Eye Chillies

Chinese Flowering Cabbage

Jaggery (Palm Sugar)

Tamarind Pods

Tofu

Watercress

Bamboo Shoots

Bamboo shoots are the tender young shoots of the bamboo plant. They can be either bitter or sweet, depending on what climate they were grown in. They are available fresh or canned. If using fresh, remove the outer sheath of the shoot and cut lengthwise. Boil in water for about 25 minutes or until tender. Canned shoots can be used directly from the can.

Banana Leaves

In Asia, banana leaves are used decoratively on plates for serving food or as a wrapper when grilling or steaming food. The leaf gives off a wonderful aroma when cooked and imparts a distinctive fragrance to the dish. In Asia, banana leaves are available fresh, but may only be available frozen in some Western countries. Fresh banana leaves should be scalded over an open flame so they are pliable and won't tear as easily. If frozen, defrost at room temperature, then gently peel apart. Frozen leaves need not be scalded.

Bean Sprouts

The bean sprouts used in Myanmar are from the mung bean. They are full of vitamins and need only light cooking. Sprouts have a short shelf life and should be consumed within a few days purchase. Discard any that are limp and have brown spots.

Bird's Eye Chillies

Bird's eye chillies are small, but they pack a lot of punch in terms of heat. Use gloves when handling chillies as they can cause a burning sensation on skin. Seeding the chillies will help reduce the heat.

Chilli Oil

Chilli oil is made from cooking dried chillies, onions and garlic in vegetable oil. It is available in bottles from the supermarket. Store refrigerated or at room temperature and always use with a clean dry spoon to avoid spoilage.

Chinese Flowering Cabbage

This vegetable has dark green leaves and may spot tiny, yellow flowers. Flowering cabbage has a light and sweet flavour, and both the leaves and stems can be eaten. Rinse well and cook lightly to retain its flavour and crunch.

Dried Black Beans

These are black soy beans that have been fermented and preserved in salt. They are very salty and have a distinctive taste and smell that can take some getting used to. I use dried black beans to substitute for dried fermented soy beans (*hto nao*) that are only available in Myanmar. *Hto nao* is a common seasoning used in Shan cooking. I have found that roasting black beans and then pounding them into a fine powder produces a similar flavour. Dried black beans can be found in most Asian markets. Store in a cool, dark and dry place and they should last indefinitely.

Fish Sauce

Two types of fish sauce are available—Thai or Vietnamese. Both are pungent in taste and are widely used throughout Asia. Fish sauce can range in colour, from light brown to deep brown, and intensity. According to local lore in Myanmar, the lighter coloured fish sauce is considered better. Store in a cool, dark place.

Jaggery (Palm Sugar)

Jaggery is an unrefined sugar obtained from certain palm trees. It is available in both liquid and solid form and can range in colour from light brown to dark brown. It has a fragrant caramel flavour and is used to flavour many Southeast Asian desserts and snacks.

Pork Rind

Pork rind is also known as pork scratching or pork crackle. It is made from pig skin and is popular eaten as a crispy snack. In Myanmar, pork rind is served as a side dish with curries and noodle dishes.

Rice Noodles (Vermicelli)

Rice noodles are ubiquitous throughout Asia. They can be made from either brown rice flour or white rice flour and vary in thickness from fine to broad. Rice noodles are available fresh, frozen or dried. Fresh and frozen noodles need only be blanched to cook them, while dried noodles need to be soaked to soften before cooking.

Salted Fish

Salted fish is a sun-dried fish, with a pungent and salty flavour. In Southeast Asian cooking, salted fish is typically cut into small pieces before cooking.

Salted Soy Beans

Salted soy beans are sometimes also known as yellow bean sauce. It is available in bottles from most supermarkets. The beans can range in colour from light to dark brown and may be whole or mashed, and packed in a thick liquid. If properly refrigerated after opening, salted soy beans will keep indefinitely.

Spring Onion (Scallion)

Spring onions are also known as scallions or green onions. They have a mild flavour. When cooking with spring onions, it is best to add them last since they cook quickly. Trim the bottom ends off and rinse well before using.

Sticky (Glutinous) Rice

When cooked, this type of rice takes on a sticky texture, hence its name. It can be easily differentiated from regular long grain rice by its opaque white colour. When cooked, it becomes translucent. Sticky rice is used both in sweet and savoury dishes.

Tamarind

The tamarind tree is indigenous to East Africa but is now grown in Southeast Asia and India. It has long brown pods that contain a sour-acidic pulp. Tamarind is available in various forms—as pods, canned paste, blocks or concentrate.

Tofu

Also know as bean curd, the more commonly known Chinese or Japanese tofu is made from soy milk and set with a coagulant. The recipes in this book make use of firm or compressed tofu as a substitute for yellow tofu which is found only found in Shan state. Unlike Chinese or Japanese tofu, Shan yellow tofu is made from yellow split peas. A recipe for yellow tofu is provided on page 105.

Turmeric

A member of the ginger family, turmeric, like ginger is available in powder form and can also be used fresh. Turmeric has a bitter and pungent flavour and is known for its vivid yellow-orange colour which also serves to add colour to food. Beware that turmeric stains everything from clothing to silverware.

Watercress

Watercress is a small green leafy plant known for its peppery, tangy flavour. It is rich in calcium and vitamin C and can be used in salads, soups and stir-fries. Watercress should be stored refrigerated in a plastic bag or in a glass of water (stems down) to prevent wilting or yellowing. It is highly perishable and should be consumed within a day or two of purchase.

Weights and Measures

Quantities for this book are given in Metric, Imperial and American (spoon and cup) measures. Standard spoon and cup measurements used are: 1 tsp = 5 ml, 1 Tbsp = 15 ml, 1 cup = 250 ml. All measures are level unless otherwise stated.

Liquid and Volume Measures

Metric	Imperial	American
5 ml	$^1/_6$ fl oz	1 teaspoon
10 ml	$^1/_3$ fl oz	1 dessertspoon
15 ml	$^1/_2$ fl oz	1 tablespoon
60 ml	2 fl oz	$^1/_4$ cup (4 tablespoons)
85 ml	$2^1/_2$ fl oz	$^1/_3$ cup
90 ml	3 fl oz	$^3/_8$ cup (6 tablespoons)
125 ml	4 fl oz	$^1/_2$ cup
180 ml	6 fl oz	$^3/_4$ cup
250 ml	8 fl oz	1 cup
300 ml	10 fl oz ($^1/_2$ pint)	$1^1/_4$ cups
375 ml	12 fl oz	$1^1/_2$ cups
435 ml	14 fl oz	$1^3/_4$ cups
500 ml	16 fl oz	2 cups
625 ml	20 fl oz (1 pint)	$2^1/_2$ cups
750 ml	24 fl oz ($1^1/_5$ pints)	3 cups
1 litre	32 fl oz ($1^3/_5$ pints)	4 cups
1.25 litres	40 fl oz (2 pints)	5 cups
1.5 litres	48 fl oz ($2^2/_5$ pints)	6 cups
2.5 litres	80 fl oz (4 pints)	10 cups

Dry Measures

Metric	Imperial
30 grams	1 ounce
45 grams	$1^1/_2$ ounces
55 grams	2 ounces
70 grams	$2^1/_2$ ounces
85 grams	3 ounces
100 grams	$3^1/_2$ ounces
110 grams	4 ounces
125 grams	$4^1/_2$ ounces
140 grams	5 ounces
280 grams	10 ounces
450 grams	16 ounces (1 pound)
500 grams	1 pound, $1^1/_2$ ounces
700 grams	$1^1/_2$ pounds
800 grams	$1^3/_4$ pounds
1 kilogram	2 pounds, 3 ounces
1.5 kilograms	3 pounds, $4^1/_2$ ounces
2 kilograms	4 pounds, 6 ounces

Length

Metric	Imperial
0.5 cm	$^1/_4$ inch
1 cm	$^1/_2$ inch
1.5 cm	$^3/_4$ inch
2.5 cm	1 inch

Oven Temperature

	°C	°F	Gas Regulo
Very slow	120	250	1
Slow	150	300	2
Moderately slow	160	325	3
Moderate	180	350	4
Moderately hot	190/200	375/400	5/6
Hot	210/220	410/425	6/7
Very hot	230	450	8
Super hot	250/290	475/550	9/10

Abbreviation

tsp	teaspoon
Tbsp	tablespoon
g	gram
kg	kilogram
ml	millilitre